For Margot, and Ben, and of course for Wendy.
And for all lovers of gardens,
who feel beckoned to Wendy's Secret Garden.

Miniature drawing of Brett's bonsai Moreton Bay fig tree,
by Wendy Whiteley, circa 1970.

WENDY WHITELEY

AND THE

SECRET GARDEN

JANET HAWLEY

Photography by
Jason Busch

LANTERN

an imprint of
PENGUIN BOOKS

Contents

Key to sculptures and found objects

1. Joel Elenberg, *Head*, 1972, bronze
2. Ian Marr, slate slab
3. *Pinder's snake*
4. Margaret Olley's fountain
5. Robert DuBourg, white Carrara marble

6. Brett Whiteley, *Nude*,1962
7. *Lovers*
8. Tricycle
9. Railway signal
10. Scooter
11. *Kingo's lady*, beside hand basin

12. Garden prize urn
13. Wheelbarrows
14. Tiny barrow
15. Rusty wheelbarrow
16. Rusty things
17. Ruben's Hill End cairn

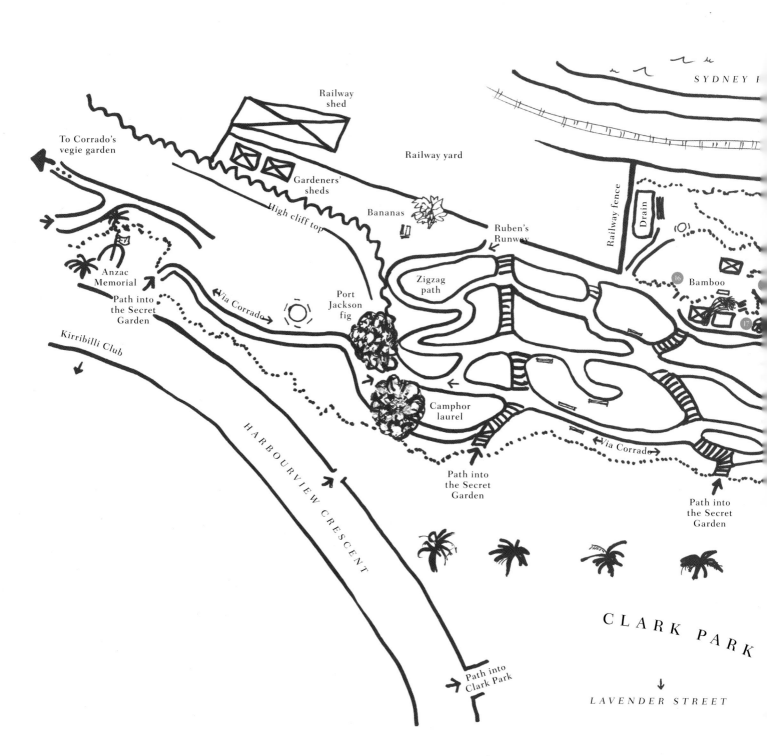

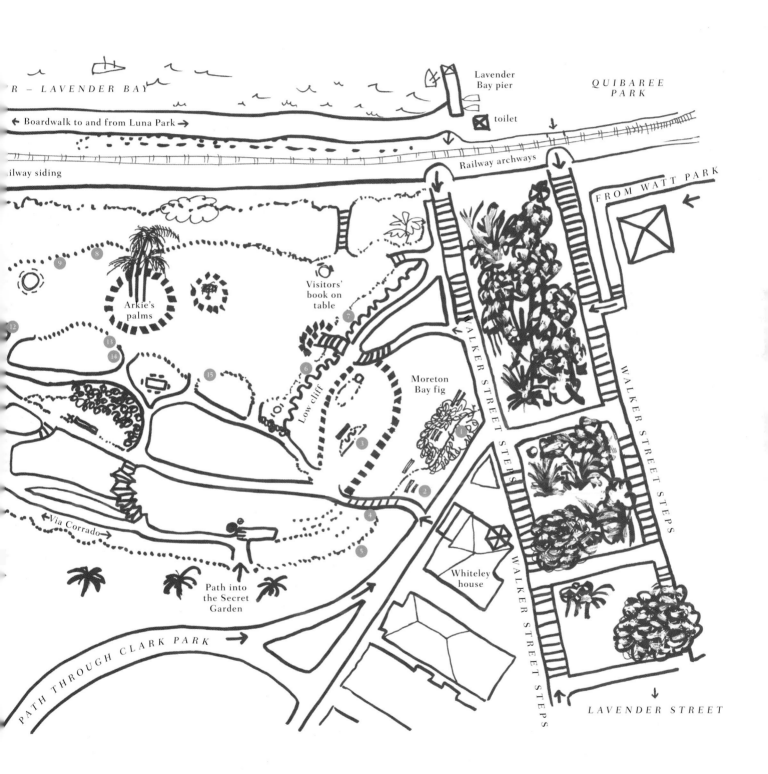

R – LAVENDER BAY

Lavender
Bay pier

QUIBAREE
PARK

← Boardwalk to and from Luna Park →

toilet

ilway siding

Railway archways

FROM WATT PARK

Visitors'
book on
table

Arkie's
palms

WALKER STREET STEPS

WALKER STREET STEPS

Moreton
Bay fig

Low cliff

Via Corrado →

Whiteley
house

Path into
the Secret
Garden

WALKER STREET STEPS

PATH THROUGH CLARK PARK →

LAVENDER STREET

SHARP

WENDY'S SECRET GARDEN

Great public gardens give identity to an area. Wendy's Secret Garden is giving another strong strand of identity to Lavender Bay.

Introduction

Wendy Whiteley

Everyone needs a Secret Garden in their life, a place to quietly contemplate and dream. I've loved making this garden; it has been a great gift to my life. It allowed me to find myself again and it is my gift to share with everybody. I've never owned it, but I do feel as if I am its mother. I am very protective of it.

Right in the heart of the garden is an old thick clump of green and white variegated bamboo, which took on a special meaning when I discovered it growing amongst the rubble. This immediately evoked strong memories of my own childhood secret garden in my mother's backyard in Lindfield. The bamboo clump I used to hide inside beside the creek, and where I read the book *The Secret Garden*, was a place where I could have my own thoughts and daydreams.

It's extraordinary how many people have told me they too had a childhood secret garden, a place no grown-ups knew about, somewhere they could go to escape the adult world when they felt misunderstood or lonely. A place to dream, make plans, be alone and feel safe in a secret cubby.

It has been a long journey for me making this garden. After Brett's death in 1992, followed by the loss of our darling daughter Arkie, who loved and contributed to the idea, I slowly turned an ugly wasteland into this beautiful sanctuary.

Loss is something all people end up dealing with one way or another. Sometimes loss can seem too much to bear, but we must allow ourselves time to get through the stages of grieving. The amazing thing about life is that deep sadness can, in its own time, eventually lead you on a path to renewal and discovery.

Over the years, the Secret Garden has grown larger and larger as we pushed further into the rubble, transforming it into a glorious place for all to share. This garden is a place that brings everybody great joy, fleeting moments of ecstasy and a renewed love of life.

Yet as beautiful and widely loved as the now not-so-Secret Garden has grown, it remains extremely vulnerable. I would dearly love for it to be made secure, so it can remain everyone's Secret Garden forever.

This book has been another journey. I have deepened my friendship with the author Janet Hawley and entrusted her with the garden's story. She has been, over the years, a stalwart supporter of it and me, for which I am extremely grateful.

I have made new friends; the wonderful photographer Jason Busch, and, at Penguin, Julie Gibbs, Daniel New and Nicole Abadee. Old friend Joanna Collard has come to the rescue and been an invaluable help.

The people who have worked with me over the years to create the garden, in particular Corrado and Ruben, without whom it could not have existed, have my eternal gratitude. To all my friends for their patience and support: I love you.

Wendy

CHAPTER 1

Optical Ecstasy

Brett Whiteley
Drawing, Lavender Bay, circa 1980s
Ink on paper, 30 cm x 21.5 cm
Private collection © Wendy Whiteley

(**WW**) 'I only found this ink drawing of
Brett's quite recently, when I was going
through one of his old catalogues.
This drawing hasn't been published
before. Brett had just sketched it on
the back of the last page.'

The view from Wendy's balcony.

(**WW**) 'It's amazing to look at all of this
now and think that over twenty-three
years I have turned an overgrown dump
of landfill into this glorious garden. It
still jolts me to think that until 1893,
this same piece of land was a beautiful
Sydney Harbour beach cove. It is tragic
that the cove was buried in landfill for
the sake of a railway line which became
redundant thirty-nine years later, when
the Harbour Bridge was built.

'But it's a redeeming triumph that
this land is now a much-loved garden.
I hope and pray the Secret Garden will
be allowed to stay here for the public,
permanently.'

W

hen you stand at the top entrance of Wendy Whiteley's Secret Garden, under the sprawling boughs of the giant Moreton Bay fig tree, place your foot on the first narrow step leading down and grip the bush-branch handrail, you instantly leave the ordinary world behind.

It seems as if you've stumbled upon someone's very private world, or discovered some wonderful secret, as you glimpse the strangely enchanting garden that lies below.

It looks and feels like a treasured love garden. Even if you know nothing of the history of Wendy Whiteley's alchemy, turning private grief and a disused dumpland into a Garden of Eden, you can sense the heartfelt love that's been poured into creating this cherished place.

The allure of Wendy's garden also draws from the striking juxtapositions of its location. True to its name, the Secret Garden lies almost hidden inside a winding valley which nestles alongside tranquil Lavender Bay. Surrounding it are grand-scale statements: the open blue of Sydney Harbour, the dramatic Harbour Bridge span, Luna Park's giant Ferris Wheel, the high rise wall of North Sydney office and apartment towers, and the formal sweeping green lawns of Clark Park.

The approach to the Secret Garden through Clark Park – a handsome though impersonal council park, with pragmatic, low maintenance lawns, bitumen paths, sturdy benches and a row of Canary Island palms – provides a perfect prelude to the surprise awaiting below.

The Secret Garden's ambience is totally different. Delightfully personal, intimate and quirky, with sculptures, a cheeky cupid fountain and high maintenance, intricate planting all lovingly cared for, as well as friendly patches of parsley, rocket, basil, tomatoes and strawberries thoughtfully planted beside picnic tables to pluck.

Little wonder that so many people over the years have hovered on the narrow top steps, asking Wendy or her gardeners, 'Can we come in here, is this garden private?' Wendy always answers with an amicable smile, 'Well, I don't own it; I'm just fixing it up, so I suppose you can all come in just like I do.'

Visitors soon love the feeling of being cocooned inside the Secret Garden, protected inside a mind-calming, leafy, flower-daubed and bird-chirping retreat, before they emerge to face the hectic modern world again.

It's hard to believe today, but once upon a time, this Secret Garden site was a picturesque harbour beach surrounded by sandstone cliffs. In 1890, the deep V-shaped inlet beach was buried in landfill, to enable the railway line to travel across the mouth of Lavender Bay.

Nowadays there'd be a massive outcry against such environmental sacrilege, but in 1890 it went ahead. The yawning rubble valley between the railway line and Clark Park became an overgrown, unused wasteland for the next century.

In 1992, Wendy Whiteley awakened its new incarnation when she began making her Secret Garden.

'Well, I don't own it, I'm just fixing it up; so I suppose you can all come in just like I do.'

(*WW*)

Optical Ecstasy

Brett at the opening of his 1970 exhibition at the Bonython Gallery, Paddington, standing in front of *The American Dream*, 1968–1969. This was the first time the iconic painting had been shown in Australia.

(*WW*) 'Brett's wearing a Russian-style black felt jacket with fur around the neck which I bought him. That's his post-Fiji hair – the biggest his hair ever got!'

'*We'd fallen in love with quiet, secluded Lavender Bay on our return to Australia.*'

(*WW*)

I first met Brett and Wendy Whiteley on the opening night of his tour-de-force exhibition in Sydney in 1970, when the boy wonder of Australian art returned home as a thirty-year-old art rockstar, after ten years living abroad.

Whiteley had earlier travelled to Italy on a scholarship, then on to London where he rapidly made a successful career, with Wendy, the talented art student sweetheart who'd become his wife/model/muse, always by his side. At twenty-four he was the youngest artist to be collected by the Tate Gallery. The couple with their toddler daughter Arkie had spent two frenetic years in New York on a Harkness Fellowship, then returned home via a calmer painting sojourn in Fiji.

Brett Whiteley had morphed into Australia's first artist as rockstar. The media heralded him on his homecoming as our new Picasso, Mick Jagger, Bob Dylan and art messiah all rolled into one. Whiteley looked the part, with his fiery eyes peering from a halo of tightly curled ginger hair, wiry body and edgy mannerisms. Wendy was his drop-dead gorgeous, sexy goddess wife; a vision of mysterious beauty with dark ringlets cascading around her cornflower blue eyes, her figure garbed in strikingly original clothes and cloche hats.

The exhibition at the Bonython Gallery in Paddington was a phenomenon, the like of which the Australian art world had never seen before. Every art connoisseur, gallery socialite, art hippy and hanger-on was trying to push through the door.

Whiteley's huge, enticing heaven-and-hell paintings filled the walls, whilst the gallery resounded with recorded birdsong, shrilling cicadas, a screaming siren. A bonfire blazed in the courtyard.

The centrepiece was his eighteen-panelled *The American Dream*, which he'd painted during a deranged, whisky-fuelled year in New York, still wanting to believe that art could change world politics. A flashing red ambulance siren light wailed in the centre of this painting, and I watched, mesmerised, as an angelic-faced girl in a crocheted cap fixed her staring eyeballs right against the spinning light. The Fiji island paintings, by contrast, were sheer romantic loveliness, a lyrical release after the exhaustion of New York.

Wendy floated around the gallery in a long dress, the supreme goddess. Brett, who meticulously planned his exhibitions and openings, wanted Wendy to cook octopus on the bonfire, but the box of octopus had gone missing. Arkie, then five, was happily jumping up and down on black velvet floor cushions, crying out, 'Ark, Ark'. She took a woman's hand and pointed to a dot in a painting, brightly saying, 'That's me!'

The Australian, where I then worked as a rookie journalist, was holding the front page for a story I'd phone in. Steered into a private room to interview the art god, I saw Brett sitting like a statue, with his face staring rigidly ahead. Notebook poised, I asked my first question. His face remained immobile, hewn in stone. I tried three more questions but the statue remained silent. My stomach churned.

Suddenly his mouth opened, and an explosion of disconnected words swirled out. I couldn't understand him; it was my first encounter with extreme Brett-speak. I caught the word 'infinity' amidst the splatter. It was dazzlingly impressive, but terrifying in terms of the story I had to file.

Wendy, Brett and Arkie, aged five, caught unawares by the press on their return by ship to Australia in late 1969.

(**WW**) 'After New York we spent about six months in Fiji. We planned to return there after the show in Sydney, but the police busted Brett in Suva, where they found a bit of opium in our room. The irony was that we didn't even know what to do with it, whether to cook it or smoke it, so Brett tried eating it and made himself sick. We were tossed out of Fiji, and Brett was banned for life. The Australian media immediately labelled us mad artists and druggies. It was the sixties and seventies, the starting era of the cult of the celebrity, and we fitted the outlandish image!'

Brett was off the planet on nerves or lord knows what that night. In later years when I knew Brett well, and got the knack of Brett-speak, I found him the most lucid, revealing and uninhibited person to talk to, with a streak of wicked playfulness. His normal state was restless high energy, like a moth dancing around a flame.

My next encounter with the Whiteleys came three years later, when I was in the 1973 Royal Tour press corps covering Queen Elizabeth II's visit to open the Sydney Opera House. The Royal Yacht *Britannia* was moored in Sydney Harbour, and Brett and Wendy were amongst the cultural stars invited on-board to a supper party hosted by the Queen and Prince Philip.

Some forty years on, I found my report and read some of it to Wendy.

> Some avowed artist-republicans had gone to extraordinary lengths to prepare for the party. Brett Whiteley's beautiful wife Wendy, admitting, 'I'm hardly a royalist, but I'd love to see inside *Britannia*', designed a stunning grey silk velvet harem pants and turban outfit, tucked into Charles Jourdan grey boots.
>
> Brett spent $300 buying a new French royal blue suit and wore his signature frangipani in his buttonhole.
>
> He even took the Queen a present – an etching he'd made looking out from his Lavender Bay home onto Sydney Harbour, with a boat at Circular Quay looking remarkably like *Britannia*. It was rolled and tied with a bow of grey velvet scrap material from Wendy's harem pants …

Wendy listened with amusement, nodding.

'We'd fallen in love with quiet, secluded Lavender Bay on our return to Australia. It's what made us stay, rather than head back overseas again. Brett called it optical ecstasy,

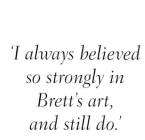

*'I always believed
so strongly in
Brett's art,
and still do.'*

(WW)

to be gazing through palms and frangipani trees at the harbour, the Bridge and the Opera House; all soaked in a wonderful quality of light. We really felt we'd come home.'

The two decades the Whiteleys lived as a family in Lavender Bay inspired an enormous creative output from Brett, who painted with a poetic sumptuousness acknowledged as his masterful, mature period. The political and social consciousness that crept into earlier works was left aside, and he turned his concentration to works of beauty.

He painted sublime, Matisse-inspired interiors of their Lavender Bay home, looking out through windows onto flowering mauve jacarandas, the Moreton Bay fig, three slender cabbage tree palms by the jetty, the Sydney Harbour Bridge and Opera House, swooping birds, scudding boats and the changing harbour scenes. Often Wendy or part of her curvaceous body was in the painting; or a sensual image of Brett and Wendy making love.

Brett painted the harbour in every light, from glorious ultramarine blue, to burning orange sunsets, to limpid silvery-grey rainy days. Whiteley's lyrical Sydney Harbour paintings soon became renowned as the new symbols of Australia's identity. In 1978, Whiteley won all three of the country's major art prizes: the Archibald, Wynne and Sulman.

However, he left no images of Wendy's Secret Garden, as during his lifetime the site was an uninviting morass of overgrown rubbish and landfill.

Brett Whiteley's artworks are a visual diary of his life, which was entwined with Wendy's from when he was seventeen and she was fifteen, and Wendy's influences on his life were manifold.

It took some time to be acknowledged – such is the lot of artists' wives – but the ambience in Brett Whiteley's paintings of relaxed, alluring interiors, the placement of sofas, plump cushions, pictures, sculptures, quirky *objets d'art*, an open book, a vase of flowers, a mirror, is all the work of Wendy, the supreme curator.

Wendy has an innate, unstoppable ability to curate any space with a highly original eye, be it an interior, a courtyard, or her own, now vast living artwork – the Secret Garden.

Or indeed, her own body. Brett often said that Wendy had the perfect face and body for the erotic forms he loved to paint. An artist herself, she knew how to pose in a languid sensual manner, be it on a sofa or the sand, or in a bath. The effortless way she slides the contours of her body, propping her head on an elbow or tucking up a supple leg, whether she's sitting and talking, or posing for a photographer – it's all just part of her, not an affectation.

Although Brett and Wendy always seemed joined at the hip, Wendy remained a strong person in her own right. Opinionated, sharply intelligent, charming, funny and warm, with a wide-ranging knowledge of art, she was a lively match for Brett at any level.

But crucially, Wendy understood the inherent complexities of the species 'highly creative artist': Brett's ego, risk-taking and need for success, the gnawing self-doubts, the ferocious drive putting everyone and everything aside when the work was flowing. Wendy knew the pitfalls of being the artist's wife/model/muse but willingly took the role because 'I always believed so strongly in Brett's art, and still do.'

Brett knew he'd hit gold when he married Wendy, proclaiming, 'If ever I have a retrospective, it will be a testament to Wendy – to my relationship with her'.

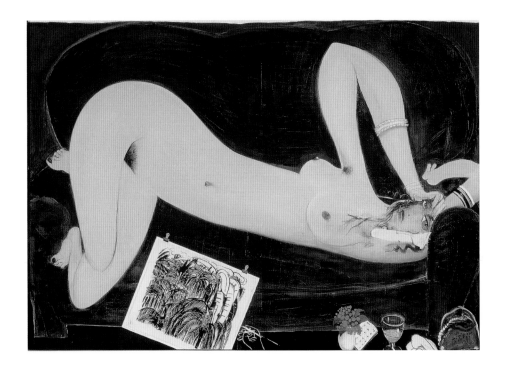

Brett Whiteley
Portrait of Wendy, 1984
Oil, material, pencil, charcoal,
pen and ink on paper on canvas,
150 cm x 212 cm
Private collection, Melbourne
Photo: AGNSW © Wendy Whiteley

(**WW**) 'I liked to lie on sofas to read –
but not necessarily naked. Brett
would see me and remark, "Ah, there
you are in your odalisque pose." I had
the kind of body that Brett liked to
paint, and often he painted me from
memory.

'In the bottom of this picture,
Brett's painted his own hand holding
up a sketch of palm trees outside the
window, to denote that the artist is
making this work, here at home, in
Lavender Bay.

'In a later period of nudes, Brett
used more distortion and would paint
me with elongated limbs, arms and
legs bent up like a praying mantis
insect.'

People often ask me why such an intelligent, talented and stunning woman as Wendy Whiteley stayed with Brett for so long, endured all his misbehaviour and his dark side, and has remained loyally devoted to his memory ever since he died.

I can only answer that if you'd known Brett, you would understand what a captivating person he was to be around, exploding with creativity and aura. It wasn't hard to see why he became such a powerful figure in Wendy's life.

In my long career in journalism as a feature and profile writer, interviewing the full gamut of supremely talented and charismatic people, Brett Whiteley was one of the most compelling characters I have ever known.

In all journalists' lives, certain people you interview will cross the barrier and become mutually trusted personal friends. This happened to me first with Brett, as he was the person I spent lengthy time interviewing, plus I would often see him around the art scene, as I was increasingly writing about artists. I spent a lot more time with Brett in the last four years of his life, when he was separated from Wendy and often seemed lonely for company. I grew to know Wendy much better after Brett died in 1992, and we became closer as friends.

Brett was one of those truly unique characters you only meet once in a lifetime. He looked the Hollywood vision of an art rockstar. When Brett entered a room with Wendy locked onto him like a precious ornament, the energy level lifted as all eyes swung to them.

The bravura and inventiveness in Brett's art exhibitions was liberating; his painterly visions were creating a new definition of being Australian. Brett was infectious company and people bathed in his charm; in his presence you felt fully alive, and as if you were seeing things with new eyes. He took such inquisitive pleasure in the world around him, the minutiae and the big ideas, and shared this in eager outpourings of dialogue. He loved talking about art.

It was always intriguing to witness Brett's mind unfold, as he spoke with self-analytical frankness, no matter which mercurial mood he might be in.

Brett could be warm, welcoming, genuinely concerned about everything and everyone on the planet, openly kind-hearted. He could be Peter Pan playful, the cheeky mimic and clown. Sometimes he'd show an endearing tenderness. He could be deeply thoughtful, seeing surprising connections, riffing inventive ideas with surging exuberance, riding the high as one idea sparked the next.

He could also be wilful, arrogant, autocratic, dismissive, cold, self-indulgent; a reckless risk-taker. Or blackly depressed and so bleak. There was an unknowable, dark mystery to him, this enigmatic, contradictory, edgy bundle of creativity and high risk-taking behaviour.

Brett spoke of other artists he admired: Picasso, Piero della Francesca, Van Gogh.

'I could never do that Van Goghian thing, the committed saint of the brush, living totally alone. I'm more in the Picasso mould. I work obsessively in a solitary way in my studio, but then I like to go to a café and talk and laugh, then bonk and go to sleep in a woman's arms.'

Brett Whiteley
The Jacaranda Tree
(**on Sydney harbour**), 1977
Oil on canvas, 208 cm x 456 cm
The Holmes à Court Collection,
courtesy of Heytesbury Holdings
Photo: AGNSW © Wendy Whiteley

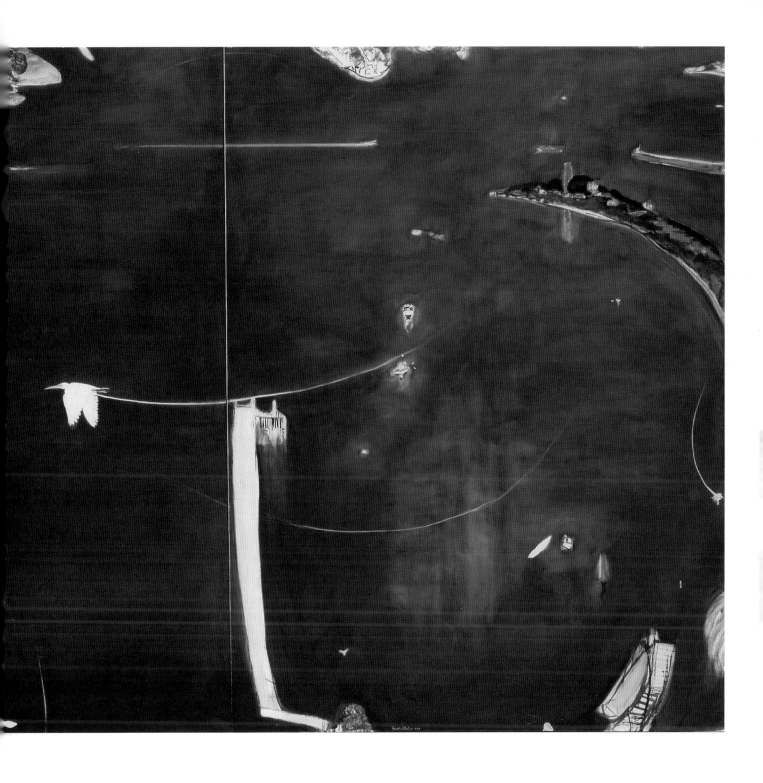

(**WW**) 'Brett has used his distinctive
Winsor & Newton French
Ultramarine to create a particular
mood. He has taken a bit of artistic
licence, because there were no
jacarandas there at the time –
I planted them much later.'

The Canary Island palms were already well established in Clark Park before Wendy started creating her garden. Sydney's CBD towers on the far side of the harbour.

Brett Whiteley
Self portrait in the studio, 1976
Oil, collage, hair on canvas,
200.5 cm x 259 cm
Art Gallery of New South Wales
Purchased 1977
Photo: AGNSW © Wendy Whiteley

*'I was very vulnerable,
and it was too
dangerous for me to be
living with Brett when
he was constantly
using heroin, and
wanting me to be using
again with him.'*

(ww)

Brett continues, 'I've always been into co-dependency. I've had the most intense interconnect-edness with Wendy since I was seventeen. We were so absorbed in each other that we rocketed off in our own satellite into our own orbit. I hope I can achieve the maturity to go on creating new work into my old age, keep up the invention, the way Picasso did.'

He also observed how many gifted people 'shipwreck' their own lives.

Brett believed in dichotomy; whatever state exists, the opposite soon arrives. In 1974, into the seemingly blissful domestic scene at Lavender Bay, came a dark intruder, heroin.

'We were both stupidly naïve when we started using heroin,' Wendy admits. 'It was a new thing that came into Sydney with American soldiers on leave from the Vietnam War, and we were always into experimenting with new ideas. Brett was such a speedy person, like an ADHD kid, and alcohol or marijuana made him speedier. Heroin calmed him down; he loved that sensation of floating away from all troubles after a heroin hit. We had this demented belief that we could use heroin every now and again, and escape the consequences. We had no concept that we'd become addicts, and that heroin would rule and ruin our lives.'

Brett's inability to give up heroin, when Wendy (after many failed attempts) successfully quit drugs forever in 1987, forced their separation.

'I was very vulnerable, and it was too dangerous for me to be living with Brett when he was constantly using heroin, and wanting me to be using again with him,' Wendy explains. 'I wasn't going to let Arkie down again; she was distraught at her parents' addiction.'

Brett moved to live in his Surry Hills studio in 1988. Torrid arguments about his heroin use, Brett's affair with a woman twenty years younger, Janice Spencer, whom he'd met at Narcotics Anonymous meetings, plus lawyers getting involved on both sides, escalated to divorce in 1989.

In 1989 I began a series of interviews with Brett, published in *Good Weekend* magazine, which led to two book proposals that we began discussing. One was a book on his portraits – I'd gone to see Wendy about this too, as she was the subject of so many of them.

Brett often seemed a lonely figure, hungry for a long conversation and a home-cooked meal, when I'd go to his studio or a café to meet him. He looked uncomfortable and incomplete without Wendy in his life.

He was ending his on-off relationship with Janice, with Brett and others remarking that it was impossible for anyone to measure up to Wendy. He admitted he missed Wendy's dynamic mind, challenging conversation, domestic and social *savoir faire*, and curatorial skills. He also needed Wendy's sharp, critical eye editing his work, as he wasn't often painting well.'What's gone wrong with Brett Whiteley's work? No Wendy,' was a frequent comment in his last years.

Brett working on *Self Portrait in the Studio*, winner of the Archibald Prize in 1976.

'I never bullshitted Brett about his work or drenched him with feel-good flattery, I always told him the truth,' says Wendy. 'And Brett always said that he trusted my eye.'

Despite being newly divorced, their property settlement was never completed, and they were constantly in touch. 'Brett was always ringing me wanting me to rescue him; he'd fallen asleep with a cigarette and burnt the bed, he needed help with something … so I'd go over and obsessively start tidying up the place, then we'd have another blazing argument about heroin,' says Wendy.

'Once I went over and found Brett sitting on the studio floor, hopelessly doped and hunched over a picture of a bird he was trying to draw. Brett looked so tragic, the quality of the drawing was tragic, and I pleaded with him to stop heroin or he'd soon be dead.'

In late 1991, Brett and Wendy went on a two-week reunion holiday in Queensland. 'Brett asked me to join him,' Wendy recalls, 'and we had an affectionate time together. He'd been going through withdrawal and wasn't very well, so I was worried and looking after him. We spent a lot of time just enjoying each other's company; talking, walking the beach, driving through the hinterland looking at things, and stopping while Brett made some sketches. Brett rang Arkie in London to say we were sorting things out and getting back together; it was all lovely.'

When they returned from that holiday, I received a phone call from Brett with such reinvigorated joy bubbling in his voice, wanting to tell his good news.

'I've been away with Wendy having peace talks,' he began. 'The insanity of our civil war had to end. We've come to construction, rather than destruction.

'We were both caught up in the war machine, fighting over the property settlement, both of us with lawyers behind us, guns blazing. I knew that every painting I did for the next four years would be for the lawyers; I was heading into pure insanity through my own wilfulness.

'You don't spend almost forty years with someone, then destroy everything. Even in the madness of war, after an hour, openings of understanding can appear. We're finding our own way now, it's so good. And I'm straight again, this time I'm staying clean. I wake up in the morning and drink twelve glasses of water and have no impurities in my body! I'm going to spend half my time at Lavender Bay and half at the studio, and Wendy can have more of her own space. We're working it out again.'

'So, can I write the big reunion story?' I asked tentatively.

'Oh Jesus, not yet, this is only asparagus days,' Brett replied, but sounding so confident and hopeful. 'Wait for the rainforest to grow.'

I always feel so wistful recalling that conversation, as tragically Brett's metaphorical rainforest never grew.

The longed-for dream of Brett breaking heroin's grip never happened. His strength, bravado and bold imagination all seemed to be tiring, he often looked haggard, his body wasn't bouncing back the way it used to. He'd become increasingly isolated and left it so late to escape.

'I never bullshitted Brett about his work or drenched him with feel-good flattery, I always told him the truth'

(WW)

(*JH*) 'In 1990 I had written a cover story on Brett, entitled "The Warrior Prince of Art". (Lloyd Rees had anointed him thus, in his last letter to Brett. The two artists were close friends.) The story detailed Brett's chaotic struggle since his separation from Wendy, and his desperate attempts to restore some balance into his life. Brett drew a symbolic sketch of himself trying to juggle seven balls in the air, and gave it to me with a thank you note.'

LEFT Brett's drawing for Janet Hawley, the author.

TOP RIGHT Brett in Byron Bay, wearing a favourite frangipani brooch on his cap.

BOTTOM RIGHT Brett with the author in a café in Byron Bay, 1990.

'It's an incredible tragedy. We always expected it could happen at any time, yet hoped it wouldn't.'

(*WW*)

Optical Ecstasy

22

At 6 a.m. on June 15, 1992, I was on my way to Sydney Airport in a taxi, which stopped at the Taylor Square traffic lights, on the corner of Bourke and Oxford Streets, outside the old brick Darlinghurst Police Station.

On the footpath, I witnessed a chilling sight. Two ravaged young male heroin addicts pushed up their sleeves and shared a full syringe. One pumped half the syringe's contents into his forearm, then handed it to the other man, who plunged the remainder into his arm. So desperate was their craving, they were oblivious to their audience of lined-up cars, and to the police station on the opposite side of the road.

The lights changed and my taxi drove on, but I felt a stark premonition on that wintry morning, thinking of Brett in his nearby Surry Hills studio and wondering how he was.

Next morning I flew back from my assignment, to an urgent message from my editor that Brett Whiteley had been found dead in a motel on the New South Wales south coast. He'd left his studio and driven south to Thirroul, a ritual place he'd go to detox, but his body could no longer cope with the abuse.

I went to Lavender Bay, where a group of close friends surrounded Wendy in the sitting room. The house of sublime creativity had become a house of grief.

Dazed with shock, Wendy wept and struggled to speak. 'It's an incredible tragedy. We always expected it could happen at any time, yet hoped it wouldn't. Brett's addiction was beyond control … heroin is a deadly destroyer.'

In the weeks that followed, Wendy's grief-stricken need to regain some control in her life, to clean up a mess that she *could* clean up, found her obsessively attacking the piles of overgrown rubbish on the large landfilled valley of unused railway land at the foot of her house.

Wendy hurled herself into the forlorn site, hacking away at lantana, blackberry vines and privet, clearing up dumped bottles, rusty refrigerators, rotting mattresses, labouring till she was too exhausted to think or feel, then collapsing into sleep each night. Then doing the same, the next day and the next. Wendy never asked any authorities for permission, and no one told her to stop, so she kept going.

When Wendy slid down the side of a cliff, cutting herself on broken glass and thorns, she hired her first strong helper, Corrado Camuglia, a cheerful, pragmatic Sicilian pizza chef, who happened to be walking by.

Corrado was in for the long haul, and is still working in Wendy's garden. Wendy hired two more helpers who stayed a few years: Chantal, a backpacker from Holland, and Justin, who worked in a native plants nursery.

'The three of us worked like bulldozers in those first years, carting out rubbish and weeds, moving huge rocks,' Wendy remembers.

Wendy then hired Ruben Gardiol, a kind-hearted, multi-skilled house painter from Uruguay, who became a natural gardener. Ruben still works in Wendy's garden, and he and Corrado are the Secret Garden's two devoted long-term gardeners, who've seen it all.

Wendy and Arkie at the opening of the Brett Whiteley Retrospective at the Art Gallery of New South Wales, 1995.

The edge of the desolate dumpland began turning into a joyous guerrilla garden.

Wendy had no grand plan, but everything she touches is done with her own highly personalised sense of aesthetics. As she continued clearing the valley, terracing steep slopes, planting thousands of shrubs and trees, placing sculptures and quirky found objects, the garden became a Wendy Whiteley living canvas.

Arkie was thrilled to see Wendy pouring her artistic skills and creative energy into such a positive project in her own right, and encouraged her mother to continue.

On 12 September 2001, Arkie came to see Wendy, bearing a serious medical diagnosis. What was earlier thought to be a stomach upset caught holidaying in Bali was in fact an aggressive form of adrenal gland cancer.

Tears pool in Ruben's eyes as he says, 'I will remember for the rest of my life the two terrible events of that day. It was still September 11 in America, and we'd woken up to hear the news that planes crashed into the Twin Towers in New York. Then we learned Arkie had a very dangerous cancer.'

Three months and one week later, on 19 December, Arkie died.

The sudden death of Wendy's greatly loved daughter, her only child, at thirty-seven, was too cruel. Brett was gone, and now Arkie. There seemed little left to live for.

Numb with grief, Wendy hurled herself into the daily garden toil with even more ferocity.

Ruben and Corrado remember Wendy for a long time after Arkie's death as being very closed-in, rarely wanting to talk. If ever she smiled, they saw heart-rending sadness in her eyes.

One can barely imagine Wendy's agonised inner monologue in those early grief-wracked years, but somewhere along the way it changed.

Slowly she began to feel the sun shining on her face again, as she saw new life growing in the garden beds multiplying around her. This seems to be one of the miraculous powers of gardening; of having your hands in the earth and watching fragile seedlings or small trees burst with new life after you've tucked them into the soil. Witnessing that new growth awakens hope.

Plants, flowers and young trees were flourishing, the wasteland was becoming smaller, and her guerrilla garden was taking over. New birds were flying into the new garden. Signs of renewal were appearing everywhere.

Perhaps Brett's metaphorical rainforest was growing.

Wendy's garden became known as the Secret Garden, because it truly was a secret garden for its first decade. It grew like a wonderful secret, discovered and enjoyed only by those who ventured beyond the steep drop at the bottom of Clark Park.

As she kept expanding the garden, hiring more gardeners, and more people found the hushed romantic oasis barely five minutes' walk from North Sydney's wall of highrise office and apartment towers, it became an open secret.

'The three of us worked like bulldozers in those first years, carting out rubbish and weeds, moving huge rocks.'

(ww)

Optical Ecstasy

*'I've loved making
this garden. It's been
a great gift to my life.
It let me find myself
again, and it's my
gift to share with
the public.'*

(WW)

Optical Ecstasy

Wendy cautiously preferred that her audacious guerrilla garden remain a secret, fearing that any publicity would result in work on the garden being stopped, and fences and 'keep out' signs being erected.

By 2006, the Secret Garden was flourishing so abundantly, and Wendy and her gardeners had become so skilled at using plants, that entering the garden was like stepping into a giant Wendy Whiteley painting.

I'd been watching the progress of the garden from its beginnings, and that year, with Wendy's agreement, I wrote the first major cover story about it for *Good Weekend*, with the hope that documenting the garden would help protect it.

North Sydney's then Mayor, Genia McCaffery, along with Robert Emerson, the council's Director of Open Spaces and Environmental Services, were highly enthusiastic about Wendy beautifying the degraded site, and conducted lengthy negotiations with New South Wales RailCorp, which owns the land.

In 2008 New South Wales RailCorp granted North Sydney Council a one-year beautification lease, renewable annually, so the Secret Garden was at last legal. In 2013, New South Wales RailCorp extended the term of the beautification lease to five years, but it remains highly vulnerable, a tempting site to be sold to a developer, the Secret Garden bulldozed flat and buildings erected in its place.

Wendy has funded the entire Secret Garden from day one, pouring millions of dollars into paying for her gardeners, thousands of trees and plants, tonnes of garden materials, plus giving her own artistic skills and labour. Wendy is constantly refining and enhancing the Secret Garden, and still enlarging it by reclaiming ever more difficult slopes. Nature has thrown everything at her – torrential storms, burst drains, mini-landslides, withering droughts – but she forges ahead.

Wendy's great wish – shared by North Sydney Council – is that the New South Wales Government will pass the land over to the North Sydney Council, to remain a public garden in perpetuity. At the time of writing, 2015, this wish remains unfulfilled.

Over the years, Wendy and I have discussed documenting more fully the story of the Secret Garden in a book, with the hope that this might help to safeguard its future.

The more we talked, the more it became obvious that the book also needed to encompass the wider back-story: the intriguing history of Lavender Bay, the different incarnations of the actual site of the Secret Garden and the artists and characters who have lived around the bay through the centuries. And the remarkable Brett and Wendy Lavender Bay years, which saw an outburst of Brett Whiteley's highest artistic creativity. Everything is interlinked with the story of how the Secret Garden came into being. But it is also Wendy Whiteley's intensely personal story.

I'd grown to know Wendy in a much closer way as a personal friend in the years after Brett died in 1992, so I'd watched the evolution of the Secret Garden as a writer and a friend.

'Everyone needs
a Secret Garden in
their life, a place to
quietly contemplate
and dream. I'd dearly
love this garden to be
made secure, so it can
be everyone's Secret
Garden forever.'

(WW)

I learned to understand her many moods, when to dodge a tempest and let it die down, knowing that at the end of the day, Wendy is always fair. I admired her broad life wisdom, survival humour, and extraordinarily candid honesty about herself and her life.

I must have talked to Wendy for hundreds of hours now, whilst sitting at her kitchen dining table. It's oval-shaped, zinc-plated and usually piled with papers, letters, books, invitations, her diary, printouts of emailed requests for her help on numerous art-related matters. It's where she likes to sit and talk. Our conversations sometimes continue all day, over several cups of her favourite lapsang tea and brewed coffee. At lunchtime she'll make scrambled eggs with rocket on avocado toast and we keep talking.

Today she looks at her life through the lens of latter-day understanding, a battle veteran who's come through so many extremes of experiences, and finally found calm waters. Her real love for Brett remains, but it's a love that wears no blinkers, as you'll discover through this book.

(**WW**) 'I love strong shadows in a garden, they cast visual intrigue.'

bull-bull's nest
in avocado tree

CHAPTER 2

Wendy's Childhood Secret Garden

Brett Whiteley
Bull bull's nest in avocado tree (detail), 1976
Ink and wash, 68 cm x 101 cm
Private collection
Photo: The Beagle Press © Wendy Whiteley

As a child, Wendy's favourite book was *The Secret Garden* by Frances Hodgson Burnett. Strong-minded, bossy little Mary Lennox is orphaned and sent to live on an English estate in the care of a mostly absent uncle. Unloved and miserable, Mary discovers a neglected walled garden hidden behind a locked gate, and makes this her secret garden, her own secret world. A farm boy teaches her how to grow plants, feel kinship with birds and small animals, and she transforms her unkempt secret garden into a flowering paradise. Mary takes her uncle's sickly, sad, wheelchair-bound son into the secret garden to work beside her. As the children nurture the garden, they nurture themselves and change into healthy, happy children bursting with new life – just like their secret garden.

'That book was pivotal to me as a child,' reflects Wendy. 'I had my own childhood secret garden, my small hideaway where I'd retreat with my private thoughts and dreams, and it was vitally important to me.

'When I began making the garden at Lavender Bay, it seemed right to call it a secret garden. It started off being a small secret garden, but now it's huge and the secret is out. I've deliberately put lots of private nooks in the garden, so anyone can find a spot to use as their own secret garden, to have conversations with themselves, or just spend time there in their own special way.'

Strong-minded and quite bossy little Wendy Julius wasn't orphaned, but her father left home in mysterious, unexplained circumstances when she was six, and, apart from one brief meeting a few years later, she never saw him again.

Her mother Daphne remarried a military man, Albert McKenzie, and the family moved to a house at Lindfield, a garden suburb some twenty minutes north of Lavender Bay.

'I was about ten when we moved to Lindfield, and this is the garden I remember most,' says Wendy. 'It was a big garden that sloped down behind the house to a creek at the bottom, then up the other side to gum trees and bush. Tadpoles and frogs lived in the creek where I played, and big blue-tongued lizards sunbaked on rocks. I knew about dangerous spiders, funnel-webs and redbacks, but I'd run around in bare feet and was fearless.

'I've always had an easy intimacy with nature; I feel more comfortable being outside than inside the house. I love the smell of freshly cut grass, the feel of lying on the ground in touch with the surface of the earth, the sound and taste of rain.

'Near the creek was a large stand of bamboo, and I carved myself a little cubby inside the bamboo, as my secret garden. I had to share a bedroom with my two-year-younger sister Aileen, so my secret garden was *my place* and no one else was allowed into it!

'I was the rebellious daughter, while Aileen was the contented, good daughter. I always felt no one properly understood me because I was different and, what's more, I wanted to be different. My mother's family always thought I was a bit odd and took to calling me "Mad Wendy". I never really bonded with my stepfather. He was a good man, but a disciplinarian, so I preferred to build a romantic fantasy around my disappeared father, George Julius, known as "Gentleman George". I thought maybe my father was mad, and I'd inherited some madness from him.'

*'I had my own
childhood secret
garden, my small
hideaway where
I'd retreat with my
private thoughts and
dreams, and it was
vitally important
to me.'*

(**WW**)

*Wendy's Childhood
Secret Garden*

33

(**WW**) 'I have an illustrious family of forebears, but there is also a dark side. My great-grandfather was a famous engineer who rode into the sea and shot himself. My grandfather was a brilliant scientist, who was knighted, and my grandmother, Lady Julius, was State Commissioner of the Girl Guides. Their son, my father, was a charming rogue who ended up in jail. So, I have on the one hand a sense of great pride in their achievements, but on the other a sense of having quite a few skeletons in my closet.'

'I identified with outsiders because I always felt I was one.'

(WW)

*Wendy's Childhood
Secret Garden*

'My mother had two more children, Ian, who died from cancer in his twenties, and Caroline. Caro was only three when I left home at sixteen, then I was living overseas with Brett. So I really didn't get to know her until we came back to live in Lavender Bay. Caro is a brilliant film producer, who works for Sir Peter Jackson, the renowned New Zealand film director.'

Wendy remembers her mother Daphne as a beautiful, loving woman, always in her garden.

'It was her survival mechanism in many ways. She'd go into the garden when she wanted to be herself, so now I connect with my mother very much in that way.

'In that era of being "just a housewife", if a woman was doing something that appeared to be virtuous, like cleaning or gardening, people would leave her alone because she was fulfilling her womanly domestic role.

'Sadly, I never appreciated what my mother was doing there, nor offered to help or learn from her. I was probably irritated she was always out in the garden, and equally irritated if I was asked to rake up leaves, as I always had something more important to do.'

Young Wendy Julius would retreat to her bamboo secret garden, and daydream about her famous inventive and eccentric relatives. 'I identified with outsiders because I always felt I was one.'

Two relatives in particular fascinated her. She'd grown up hearing about her great-grandfather on her father's side, Charles Y. O'Connor (1843–1902), the visionary Engineer-in-Chief of Western Australia, whose bold scheme was to pump water, uphill, 600 kilometres from Perth to the goldfields in Kalgoorlie. 'It was to be the longest pipeline in the world, uphill – something never previously done,' relates Wendy. 'It was hugely expensive and wildly controversial; some people called C.Y. O'Connor a genius, others a madman. The scheme was almost completed in 1902, but malicious, inaccurate criticism in the press that the pipeline would never work wore him into deep depression.

'One morning he rode his horse into the sea at Fremantle, and shot himself dead. A myth grew that C.Y. O'Connor shot himself because the water didn't come through the pipe, and the next day the water flowed, but that's not true. He actually shot himself a few months before the scheme was successfully completed.

'So I always saw my great-grandfather as this tragic, romantic hero, and visualised that dramatic final image of him riding his horse into the surf, lifting his revolver to his head. Apparently he took his false teeth out and put them in his pocket before he shot himself.'

Wendy never met C.Y. O'Connor, but did meet his free-thinking artist daughter, Kathleen O'Connor (1876–1968), who sailed off to live in Paris and relished the bohemian lifestyle. 'I identified very strongly with my daring great-aunt, and she became a role model for my own artistic dreams,' Wendy admits.

Kathleen O'Connor, with her golden hair, blue eyes and penchant for wide-brimmed hats, was said to look like a woman who'd stepped out of a Manet painting. A lively individualist

who refused to be tied down, Kathleen studied art in Paris and exhibited in Paris salons, then did likewise in London.

'When I was quite young, my sister and I were very excited about going to meet our exotic great-aunt Kathleen at the Queen's Club in the city, when she was back visiting Sydney,' Wendy recalls. 'She gave me two of her paintings, still lifes of flowers.

'At school I was good at art. I had a natural facility for drawing, and when I won the David Jones Art Prize all I wanted to do was leave high school and go to art college.'

Another of C.Y. O'Connor's daughters, Eva, married George Julius, a mechanical engineer and major inventor, later to be knighted Sir George Julius.

Sir George Julius (1873–1946), Wendy's grandfather on her father's side, invented the first racecourse automatic totalisator, and was first longtime chairman of the Council for Scientific and Industrial Research, later to become the CSIRO. His father, George Alfred Julius (Wendy's other great-grandfather), was the first Anglican Archbishop of New Zealand.

'We remained very close to my Julius grandparents after my mother divorced their errant son, George Junior,' Wendy explains. 'I think they sided with my mother, as my father was a rogue. My grandparents lived in a huge house in Killara, the next suburb to Lindfield. When my sister and I visited Grandma Julius, her personal maid, called Marion, would make us pretty triangles of bread scattered with hundreds and thousands. They had a beautiful sprawling old garden with a rope swing strung from a high branch on a loquat tree.

'I loved being in the garden. I always felt safe in a garden, much safer than being locked up inside houses anywhere. I'm still like that, I can't bear being confined in small spaces, with airconditioning and no windows you can open. I have to get out of places like that.

'I've always needed an escape route, and I think drugs was an escape route for both Brett and me. It's that kind of anti-authoritarian streak.'

Wendy's strongest memories of her father, design engineer 'Gentleman George' Julius, are from the time she was four or five and living in Gordon, another North Shore garden suburb. 'I remember this charismatic, charming man, who spoiled me with lots of presents, then disappeared from my life,' says Wendy.

'Just before he disappeared, I was walking in a reserve near our Gordon house with my grandmother, and I can still see the image of her lace-gloved hand approaching to cover my eyes, when she spotted two dogs copulating in front of us. I was always escaping into that reserve. I'd see snakes and big wombats, but I wasn't frightened.'

Wendy's mother never told her daughters why she divorced their father. 'When I was thirteen, I found a pile of newspaper clippings about him hidden in her drawer,' Wendy recalls. 'It was a shattering revelation. It appears that he was an unfaithful scoundrel, having love affairs all over the place, and my mother eventually threw him out. It was hard to get a divorce in those days; you had to be caught in bed by a private detective. Well, my father was caught in bed with *two* women at the Hydro Majestic Hotel!

'I loved being in the garden. I always felt safe in a garden, much safer than being locked up inside houses anywhere.'

(**WW**)

Wendy's Childhood
Secret Garden

Wendy's parents, 'Gentleman George' and Daphne Julius.

(**WW**) 'I remember one night when I was about six hearing my parents having a huge row and my mother ordering my father to leave. He packed his bags and left our lives forever. He ended up in jail, and I remember a girl at school saying to me "Your father is in jail isn't he?" I denied it, but felt that I had betrayed him. He gained the nickname "Gentleman George" in jail, because he was well-educated and ran the prison library.'

'Well, my father was caught in bed with two women at the Hydro Majestic Hotel!'

(**WW**)

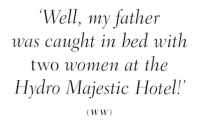
Wendy's Childhood Secret Garden

'On top of that, he was a jailbird. He'd been in prison twice for long lists of stealing from houses … And the year I found the newspaper clippings, 1954, he'd been sentenced to eight years jail for nicking a truckload of Victa rotary mowers. He claimed he'd invented the rotary mower and the patent should have been his, so he really owned them!'

A colourful account of Gentleman George Julius's life appeared at the time in Sydney's *Sun-Herald* newspaper.

The sentencing judge declared, 'It would take Shakespeare or a Zola to tell the tragedy of Julius's life'. This son of the CSIRO chairman and grandson of a New Zealand Archbishop had, by his own admission, committed some 150 robberies since he shook himself free from his father's shadow. But he was a gentleman thief. His trademark was that he always left the houses spotless, and shut the front door tight.

Patrick White, Australia's Nobel Prize-winning author, was at the same school as Wendy's father (Tudor House, Moss Vale). White was so fascinated by the story of the respectable George Julius becoming a burglar and ending up in jail for eight years that he based a character in a novel on him. Sadly, White abandoned the novel at the end of a long first draft, and never completed it.

'My father was definitely the black sheep of the family, but I identified with what I chose to see as his rebellious streak,' remarks Wendy. 'With the genes I'd inherited from all my quirky, non-conformist, defiantly individualistic forebears, I felt I really was Mad Wendy.'

Retreating to her secret garden inside the stand of bamboo, young Wendy would confide her private thoughts and yearnings to her pet dog, and to nature's ears.

'Plants are great listeners,' she reflects. 'I've been talking to plants for as long as I can remember.'

'My father was definitely the black sheep of the family, but I identified with what I chose to see as his rebellious streak...'

(*WW*)

*Wendy's Childhood
Secret Garden*

(**WW**) 'This large clump of bamboo was already growing there before I started working on the garden. It reminds me of the bamboo clump growing in my childhood garden, and how I burrowed into it and made my own secret garden. It's a very precious memory.

'The bamboo becomes very heavy when it rains and falls down, so Corrado built the frame to hold it up. It is a lovely shady spot, so we added a table and chairs.'

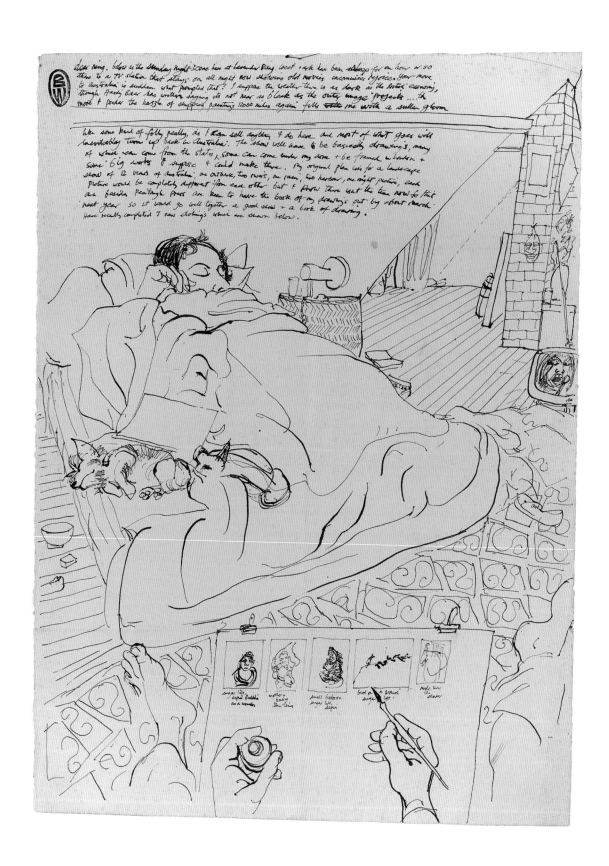

Dear Wendy, below is the Sunday night scene here at Lavender Bay. We've both been sleeping for an hour or so there to a TV station that stays on all night now showing old movies, cartoons etc. Your move to Australia is sudden - what prompted that? I suppose the weather there is as dark as the British economy, though Handy Baer has written saying its not near as bleak as the outer image projects ... the more I ponder the hassle of shipping paintings 12000 miles again fills me with a sullen gloom

like some kind of folly really, as I can sell anything I do here and most of what goes well inevitably turns up back in Australia. The show will have to be basically drawings, many of which can come from the states, some can come under my arm + be framed in london + some 'big works' I suppose I could make there. My original plan was for a landscape show of 12 views of Australia: one outback, two rivers, one rain, two harbour, one night picture, each picture would be completely different from each other but I know there isn't the time now for that and besides Pentagle Press are keen to have the book of my drawings out by about march next year so it would go well together a good show + a book of drawings. Have recently completed 7 new etchings which are shown below.

sugar lips sepia bubble acid wonders   mother + baby skin lines   small baboon sugar lips sepia   bird on a branch sugar lips   nude in the shower

CHAPTER 3

Wendy and Brett

Brett Whiteley
Letter to Ning, circa 1977
Pen and black ink on cream woven
paper, 72.7 cm x 53.1 cm
Brett Whiteley Studio Collection
Photo: AGNSW © Wendy Whiteley

(**WW**) 'Arkie, when very young,
invented the name "Ning" for Brett's
mother, Beryl. Brett and many in the
family called Beryl Ning from then on.'

Brett and Wendy in Bali, 1980.

(**WW**) 'We were in Bali with sculptor Joel Elenberg, Brett's best friend. It was a bittersweet time. Joel knew he was dying of cancer, and he wanted to die in Bali, so a group of his dearest friends and family were there with him.'

One day Brett Whiteley, the precociously talented young artist, saw this knockout beauty walking into Jericho's, a bohemian café in Sydney's Rowe Street, in tight jeans with her art folder under her arm, 'My best drawing strapped to the outside of my folder to show off,' chuckles Wendy.

Brett, then seventeen and working at Lintas advertising agency, remembered muttering to himself, 'God, I wish I could score someone like her!'

A mutual friend arranged a meeting and took Wendy to the Whiteley family home at Longueville, a harbourside garden suburb ten minutes north of Lavender Bay. The two locked eyes, welding an instant bond.

'Brett borrowed his father's car and on our first date took me to the local sketch club at Northwood, run by John Santry,' Wendy recalls. 'They had an artist's model, and Brett and I drew the nude. Some first date! I was fifteen, about to turn sixteen. We started going to the sketch club weekly. That's where I met darling old Lloyd Rees, whom Brett knew already.

'I was dazzled by Brett; the attraction between us was immediate and very powerful. He was incredibly charismatic, risky, pretty wild, and irreverent; he made me laugh and think. Brett was *different*. I'd always had a sense of myself as a romantic outsider, who wasn't going to live an ordinary life, so I was drawn to Brett, who felt the same way. Both of us had enormous energy and confidence. Brett's energy was like a coiled spring. We both wanted to jump in the deep end and just go for it.'

Physically, Brett was a tough little nugget, she says. He had ginger hair and white skin, which drove him crazy, as he loved the beach but could never get a tan; he'd just go red and get freckles.

'Brett talked in a kind of code,' Wendy continues. 'He was very speedy. He'd engage with people with a great amount of curiosity, then flick his attention to something else. Brett could never read more than half a page of a book, before his head was spinning off with some inter-connected idea of how he could turn a phrase into an image, or nick a line from the book and put it on a painting.

'Today they'd doubtless diagnose Brett as ADHD and put him on medication. Unfortunately, the only thing that gave Brett a sense of stillness was heroin. Heroin, and the behaviour it caused, drove us apart.'

Brett had grown up in Longueville, being regarded as a precocious young Picasso by both his parents, Clem and Beryl, and elder sister Frannie.

A lively little rascal, Brett was the self-appointed leader of a group of neighbourhood boys, The Hairy Balls Club, whom he'd cajole into mischief as they played in bushland, climbed trees and mucked around in small boats on the bay. Brett was famous for stealing alcohol from the local boat club and hiding it in neighbourhood chook sheds; a favourite prank was setting fire to neighbours' letterboxes. Brett's childhood friend and neighbour, Ian MacTavish, says, 'Some Longueville mothers indulged Brett as a lovable scallywag. Others regarded Brett as an utter pest. Brett was a magnetic leader of our gang.'

'I'd always had a sense of myself as a romantic outsider, who wasn't going to live an ordinary life, so I was drawn to Brett, who felt the same way.'

(*WW*)

Wendy and Brett

'We went straight to the Louvre, and seeing all the great art made me burst into tears'

(**WW**)

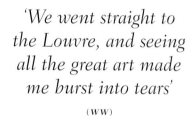

Wendy and Brett

Young Brett was such a charming little devil, with a quick tongue and winning smile, that he wheedled his way out of being blamed.

Clem Whiteley was managing director of Hoyts suburban cinemas, and his glamorous wife Beryl loved the premieres and mingling with the stars. Entertainment industry people regularly visited the Longueville home, as did artists William Dobell, William Pidgeon, and then director of the Art Gallery of New South Wales, Hal Missingham. Ian MacTavish says, 'Clem was a great dad. He'd round up the local kids and organise rugby matches in their backyard, boxing bouts, fishing and camping trips. He built Brett a fabulous billycart with an oil pump and number plate. We only had fruit boxes on wheels. Brett always wanted to win.'

At school Brett was only interested in one subject, art, and family and art world friends declared the lad showed astonishing talent.

When Wendy met Brett at his Longueville home, his mother Beryl had run off to London some months earlier on a grand love affair, leaving the rest of her family heartbroken.

Only Brett and his father Clem were then living in the house.

'After a few months of dating Brett, I moved into the house to live with them. Clem was lonely, soon regarded me as a second daughter, and I felt a lot of love for him. Brett was fiercely possessive of me, and I felt so flattered I took this as a sign of true love! Brett had no desire to go to art school, and hated me going there because I might meet other men, so he insisted I leave art school. So I did, after only eighteen months.

'Clem had a shop marketing imported patio furniture and artefacts and providing interior design services, so I began to work for him as a designer, and at night studied a design course taught by Phyllis Shillito and Peter Travis.'

MacTavish adds, 'The one abiding memory I have is Brett thundering down our Longueville street in his Fiat 500 with the sunroof open, and Wendy standing up in the car, the wind blowing through her hair.'

The larrikin in Brett was intrigued by Wendy's father, Gentleman George. When Wendy was seventeen, she managed to set up a meeting with her father in the lobby of the Hotel Australia in Sydney. 'Brett was hiding around the corner to watch, but my father didn't turn up,' Wendy recounts. 'He rang the next day to say that he had come, but when he spotted me, he felt too nervous, and left. When my father was on his deathbed, he asked a friend to tell me and my sister that he was sorry. My father's ashes are scattered in the Secret Garden, along with the ashes of my mother, her twin sister Joyce, Brett and Arkie. The ashes of our beloved dogs are here too.'

In late 1959, Brett won an Italian Government Travelling Art Scholarship and sailed to Italy. Wendy worked two jobs to save enough money to follow him, and they met up in Paris.

'We went straight to the Louvre, and seeing all the great art made me burst into tears,' Wendy remembers. 'I was nineteen, Brett was twenty-one, and it was so emotionally overwhelming seeing the actual paintings, after only looking at poor reproductions in books back in Australia.

We stood together in front of Giotto's *St Francis of Assisi Receiving the Stigmata*, and I was weeping. Seeing the quality of the paint, the scale of the works, feeling a connection with real artworks produced by the masters, was a thrilling experience to share with Brett. Love of art opened up the world to me; it gave Brett and me everything. We honed our visual intelligence together, researching, looking at a lot of art, sculpture, landscapes, absorbing and learning about form, shape, colour and texture. I've kept honing my visual intelligence all my life.'

Brett was pushing Wendy to marry him. 'He wanted to lock me to him as *permanently his*, so we married in Chelsea Registry Office in 1962. I had a frock, which I hated, and wore a hat. Brett wore a suit which he hated, and had his hair cut.

'Brett was my lover, friend and now my husband. I was totally in love with this charismatic artist with astonishing talent. He worked very hard and wanted me with him twenty-four/ seven. Brett was obsessive about his work, but artists need to be selfish about creating their work to succeed.'

Brett's two-years-older sister, arts writer Frannie Hopkirk, was devoted to her precociously talented young brother, and watched the Brett and Wendy relationship grow from the first spark.

Long ago, Frannie perceptively described the dynamics of the Brett and Wendy partnership.

'Brett was in love with Wendy from absolutely the word go,' Frannie began.

'Wendy was a sublime combination of physical beauty, intelligence and sensuality, qualities that Brett worshipped. The presence of sex around these two was unbelievable. It was in the air, an absolute dynamic, like a life force. They were locked in a mutual sexual attraction that everyone could see. It lasted for decades until drugs interfered with it, as drugs always do.

'They also had a great friendship, and exclusivity. You always felt they had a special purchase on something very exclusive when they were together. They were communicating on every level, with a look, touch, with signals, or a word. It was an all-engrossing relationship.

'Wendy was greatly loved by Brett; he loved her mind, her body, her face. When she spoke he was always listening. He was also very jealous and possessive of Wendy. He had to have Wendy placed so he always knew where she was, so she was always there for him. At the same time, Brett wanted to be free to do whatever he wished – that was just one of his many contradictions.'

Brett was an immediate success in London, exhibiting his abstract landscapes and then erotic paintings of Wendy in the bath. The distinguished Marlborough Gallery took him on and his career spiralled upwards.

Wendy would later jokingly say, after Brett had painted her nude in the bath so often, 'I must have been the cleanest artist's model in the business.'

The sixties was an exciting time to be in London. Brett and Wendy mixed with the tribe of fellow Australian artists and writers also there – Arthur Boyd, Sidney Nolan, Michael Johnson, Colin Lanceley, John Olsen, Clive James and Barry Humphries.

'He wanted to lock me to him as permanently his, so we married in Chelsea Registry Office in 1962. I had a frock, which I hated, and wore a hat. Brett wore a suit which he hated, and had his hair cut.'

(**WW**)

Wendy and Brett

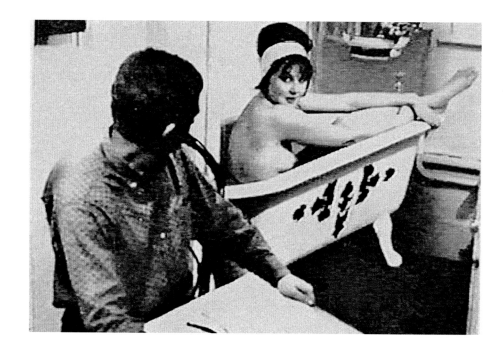

(**WW**) 'This shot was taken in London in about 1963. Brett had just done an exhibition with a lot of paintings of me in the bath, and this was publicity for the show.'

OPPOSITE (**WW**) 'A summer party at our place at Lavender Bay in about 1980. We'd all drunk rather too much, and I'm playing around, sitting on the edge of the bath.'

'I must have been the cleanest artist's model in the business.'

(**WW**)

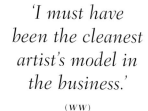

Wendy and Brett

Friends kept asking Wendy why she had given up painting, when she was so talented at art school.

'It didn't occur to me to compete with Brett,' Wendy responds. 'I had a lot of talent, but I didn't have that driven ambition artists need. Brett had the most extraordinary ambition, which I admired, and I had no desire to get in the way of it; rather I wanted to help it. I wasn't sublimating myself, no way. I was having such an exciting time working with Brett, there was always so much stuff that had to be done. I was immersed in the smell and mess of paint daily, as we always lived and had Brett's studio in the same place. We were living a life of art together, he painting, me modelling, involved, looking at art together, going to galleries, meeting other artists, having discussions, arguing, discovering. Brett trusted my eye, and I was his sounding board and critic. It was such a stimulating life and we met amazing people.

'Lord Snowdon came to photograph Brett. He was still married to Princess Margaret and we'd get invited to parties at Kensington Palace. Brett became friends with Francis Bacon and we'd visit his studio. David Hockney lived around the corner. We met Bridget Riley and most of the new generation of young British artists.

'We went to Majorca every summer, staying in Deia, and often visited Robert Graves, the wonderful writer and poet who lived there.'

In 1967 Brett won a Harkness Fellowship. With Arkie just three, they moved to New York, living for the next two years in a rooftop apartment in the legendary Chelsea Hotel, then an inexpensive haven for artists and bohemians in a rundown part of the city. They befriended Janis Joplin and Jimi Hendrix, fellow Chelsea residents at the time. Other regulars at the hotel included Bob Dylan, Arthur Miller, Andy Warhol and Leonard Cohen.

Leaving behind their frenetic life in New York, they spent five calmer months in a Fijian village, then returned to Australia and found Lavender Bay.

Photographs taken on board the ship as they arrived in Sydney marked the launch of the art world's new celebrity couple. Brett looked like a rockstar with his mass of curly hair and dark glasses. As befits the image, he'd been busted for possession of opium in Fiji.

Virtually from their early twenties the striking artstar couple Brett and Wendy Whiteley had become symbols, representing an exciting time of change in Australian contemporary history.

It was the sixties and seventies, when Australian society shook itself out of its cultural and political straightjacket and celebrated a flowering of Australian talent in all the arts – painting, film, music, along with the culinary arts and wine-making. Suddenly we had our own Australian celebrities, instead of thinking that anyone from overseas was superior. Brett Whiteley was our first home-grown artist with rockstar status. He enjoyed soaking up the fame, and Brett and Wendy rocketed to the heights of uber-celebrity and arts aristocracy.

All the world loves great lovers, and the media and public became swept up with the romance of Brett and Wendy Whiteley.

*'I wasn't a saint,
or a sinner; I was both,
so was he'*

(WW)

Wendy and Brett

'I think it was inevitable that I'd be attracted to someone quite dangerous,' Wendy reflects. 'We had a powerful intellectual and intimate connection, and I worked with Brett a very long time. Everyone wanted to see us as Australia's Scott and Zelda Fitzgerald, and I'd point out, "Look what happened to them, they self-destructed," ' remarks Wendy, wryly.

Wendy acknowledges that Brett was the great love of her life, and with the wisdom of hindsight and much self-reflection, she talks about him with remarkable frankness.

The speeding fame train that hit the young couple, mythologising them as 'genius artist and goddess muse' was inevitably distorting, she says.

'I wasn't a saint, or a sinner; I was both, so was he,' Wendy explains. 'We were both complex people in a highly complex relationship, and he and I were probably the only people who understood how it worked.

'The artist's wife role, the muse, has always existed throughout the ages. There will always be muses, feminism isn't going to change that. It's exciting, deeply intimate, and also a huge responsibility. You control them, they control you. You're caretaker, negotiator, inspirer, model; you love it, believe in its worth, carve out your own identity and survive it, or go mad and self-destruct.'

Wendy points out that a muse can sometimes be a moment, a song or a poem. Some artists say nature is their muse.

48

Brett and Wendy canoodling at a book launch for their friend, poet Robert Adamson, in Sydney in 1982.

(*WW*) 'I am wearing a beautiful embroidered Chinese robe which I bought in London at auction. It disappeared later, much to my annoyance.

'Our photographer friend William Yang was at the book launch and took these rather intimate pictures of Brett and me.'

Wendy and Brett

OPPOSITE Wendy and Brett in the studio Brett rented in an old gasworks building at Waverton, near their Lavender Bay home, circa 1972.

(**WW**) 'On the floor you can see some of Brett's preparatory work for *Alchemy*, plus a portrait of the French poet, Arthur Rimbaud.

'I used to love wearing those workman's overalls, usually with nothing underneath. But it's clearly winter as we both had jumpers on.

'Our photographer friend Greg Weight dropped into the studio to visit and took this unposed photograph.'

LEFT Wendy, Brett and Arkie in a photo studio in Fiji, 1969.

RIGHT *Portrait of Arkie with monkey doll*, circa 1970 Charcoal, brush and black ink on ivory wove paper, 73 cm x 53.8 cm Brett Whiteley Studio Collection Photo: AGNSW © Wendy Whiteley

'Being the full-time muse to an artist like Brett was a job that few women could survive,' she adds. 'I didn't survive it in the end, we both became addicts.'

To clarify one possible notion, Wendy stresses that neither Brett nor she were ever the type of heroin addicts who shot up, then lay around all day like a couple of spaced-out hippies in a filthy house. 'Even when we used heroin, we were always busy. Brett never stopped painting, and I was always busy doing my things. I was obsessive about cleaning, housekeeping, and my appearance. And, of course, caring for Arkie. Brett was an affectionate and entertaining father.'

Life with her artist husband was never dull. Brett was vain, fascinating, funny, infuriating, but never boring. As outrageous as he could be, he was also very forgivable, because of his abundant talent. Indeed, like many highly talented, high-libido-driven men, he got away with blue murder.

'I forgave Brett so often because of his artistic talent,' Wendy reflects. 'I took him back so many times because I believed so strongly in his work. I always felt a responsibility to help and protect his work. I still do, and that's why I spend so much time and energy working for the Brett Whiteley Studio at Surry Hills, to ensure it remains a vital permanent museum.'

Wendy admits that she and Brett did have 'a reasonably volatile relationship, but I loved being around him, listening to his ideas, watching to see what he'd create next. Brett's beautiful flowing line – he didn't have that at first. I had it, not Brett. He had to struggle very hard to free himself up, to be able to draw the way he wanted to, and then he became a superb draughtsman.

'Brett was always trying new ideas, learning about Chinese and Japanese art, duality, Zen, new ways of making marks, and we'd continually discuss all this.'

Depending on how his work and life were going, 'Brett could be soft, loving, listening, enveloping, or hard, rejecting and cold,' says Wendy. 'We had exciting, mad, high times, some real depths of agonising grief, pain and dissension, and in between there were acres of time when it was perfectly peaceful and right. He was working, and there was Ark and me, dogs, kids, family, a lot of love and it was just comfortable.

'Brett is absolutely woven into the fabric of my life. I spent almost forty years with him, so Brett and all his artworks are embedded in my psyche and my cells. Something is constantly happening that reminds me of him.

'I miss Brett. I don't feel rage any more, just sadness and nice thoughts … about the way he made me laugh, and how excited he'd have been about the garden, seeing this new bird or that plant. I miss his creative turn of mind and watching his creative process.'

CHAPTER 4

Discovering the Secret Garden

Brett Whiteley
Palm (for print), 1979
Brush and ink on cardboard, 101.7 cm x 71.5 cm
Brett Whiteley studio collection
Photo: AGNSW © Wendy Whiteley

Aerial view of the dense canopy of the Secret Garden, and at the head of the garden, the Whiteley home with its distinctive tower. The enormous canopy of the Moreton Bay fig is in front of the house. The railway line and boardwalk run along the edge of Lavender Bay, and Clark Park adjoins on the right.

At the time of writing, there are still no signposts leading to or in front of Wendy's Secret Garden, though after twenty-three years this may finally happen.

Wendy's gardeners, however, have been proudly wearing Secret Garden T-shirts for several years now.

The easiest way to find the main entrance is to look for the massive Moreton Bay fig tree, which stands like a sentinel guard at the top of the garden. This noble tree grows at the foot of the four-storey cream bagged-brick Whiteley house, which is another landmark with its distinctive storybook tower. There are several ways to approach the Secret Garden and many paths now lead into its seedpod-shaped circumference.

From Lavender Street, walk down the lower Walker Street stairs, turn left beneath the last house (the tower-topped Whiteley house) and continue towards the huge Moreton Bay fig. Or walk through Clark Park to the lower edge of the park's formal lawns, and several narrow paths and stairways lead down into the terraced Secret Garden.

Another dramatic approach is to come around the harbour foreshore boardwalk from Luna Park, walk under the railway viaduct and then a short distance up lower Walker Street steps. Turn right beneath the first house, the Whiteley house, and look for the huge Moreton Bay fig just ahead.

It was beneath this tree that Wendy began the Secret Garden in 1992.

'An interrupted view
is more intriguing
than a clear view.'
(WW)

———

Wendy and Brett's long love affair with this powerful sculptural tree began in 1969 when they first moved into Lavender Bay. Brett painted numerous sensually anthropomorphised versions of the tree, with its snaking buttress roots, powerful smooth trunk, sinuous branches and broad, glossy leaves.

Standing on her balcony and gazing out at the Moreton Bay fig, Wendy recalls, 'When we arrived here in late 1969, that tree wasn't even as high as our balcony. There's a photograph of Brett sitting here on the balcony in 1978, looking out over the top of the tree to a clear view of the whole harbour, the bridge span, and the three cabbage tree palms at Lavender Bay jetty that he often put in his paintings. The fig is a dear old friend, but I've looked after it rather too well. Now it's doubled in size and heavily screens our view. Sometimes I feel like yelling at it, "Would you mind just lifting your skirts a little higher please, you're blocking our old harbour views."

'But then,' she smiles philosophically, 'an interrupted view is more intriguing than a clear view.'

On the lawn in front of the Moreton Bay fig tree, Wendy has placed some sculptures that hold deep meaning for her.

Mounted on a pedestal to the right is a noble bronze sculpture of a female head, titled simply *Head,* 1972; by the late Australian sculptor Joel Elenberg.

The Moreton Bay fig now feels like the oracle of the Secret Garden, and also its guardian. It has been a revered tree since Wendy and Brett arrived at Lavender Bay, and doubtless holds many secrets of its own. Brett loved painting and drawing the fig's anthropomorphic form.

(**WW**) 'This tree has doubled in size since we moved into Lavender Bay, and its canopy is now enormous. It is extremely healthy and seems intent on growing bigger.'

'We don't do haute horticulture here! Though I do admire some very formal garden designs, it's not right for this site. This is a garden of slow reveal, which I hope visitors find exhilarating.'

(WW)

Discovering the Secret Garden

Wendy explains, 'Joel was Brett's best mate, but he died from cancer in 1980, aged thirty-two. Brett missed Joel terribly and admired his work, so this sculpture honours Joel and enduring friendship.'

Visiting American sculptor Robert DuBourg carved a second sculpture near the entrance, using a block of white Carrara marble remaining in Joel's studio.

Two sets of steps looping on either side of the Moreton Bay fig lead down into the Secret Garden. At the higher steps, an ornate, antique Italianate fountain with a chubby, winged Cupid sitting on three swans greets visitors.

The patinated metal fountain came from the rambling Paddington garden of the late Margaret Olley, a much-loved senior Australian artist. Olley affectionately called her Cupid 'that bad-tempered little Putti'. Water sprays from both the frog and tortoise perched on the Cupid's plump knees, also the shell in his hand.

'Margaret loved being in gardens, so we think she'd be pleased with her Cupid's new home here,' says Wendy.

As you walk down the steps to just below the Moreton Bay fig you are invited to pause and cast your eyes around, pondering which intriguing direction to explore first.

Perhaps the many winding paths that amble off to the left, disappearing beneath lush canopies of tree ferns and pendulous flowers shaped like angel's trumpets, as the paths traverse the more steeply terraced hindside of the valley.

Or you might descend the steps into the calm, scented spaces that weave seductively along the valley floor, like a sequence of beckoning open rooms.

The garden entices you to keep exploring around the next bend and to climb the multiple stairways and maze of paths. Rather like *Alice Through the Looking Glass*, every new fork taken builds your enjoyment and anticipation for the next mood change or visual surprise.

The Secret Garden feels far bigger than its actual measurement of just under a hectare, as it meanders up and down all sides of the curving valley, and you can't see from end to end, or side to side. Indeed, it's large enough to get lost there for several hours if you wish.

You soon realise that, as Wendy happily puts it, 'This is no Versailles, where you can see the entire garden's regular geometrical layout in one glimpse. There are no formal squares or parterres, no grand axes or *allées* for kings and courtiers to promenade through.

'We don't do haute horticulture here! Though I do admire some very formal garden designs, it's not right for this site. This is a garden of slow reveal, which I hope visitors find exhilarating.

'If I followed anyone's design philosophy, it's Capability Brown, who said "Work with the landscape, rather than against it," ' Wendy elaborates. 'This garden grew like a patchwork quilt, because that's how I made it – starting at one end, and working towards the other end.'

Wendy had no idea what she'd find, no concept of the shape of the smothered valley she would discover when she started clearing up the rubbish below the big fig tree.

'You couldn't see to the ground, it was actually quite dangerous and vaguely sinister.

'There were so many tangled morning glory vines, caves of lantana and thorny brambles growing over a century of accumulated dumped rubbish.

'I suppose if I'd owned the land or had permission, I could have brought in bulldozers, cranes and big trucks to clear the entire site first, see what we had here, and then draw up a master plan. But I didn't own the land, nor did I have permission, so I would have been promptly stopped if I'd tried that method.

'It's probably better I started naively the way I did. The railway workers and passers-by thought I was this mad bag lady in old clothes with a rag wrapped around her head, covered in mud; down there with her buckets, spade and rake, delving in the mess.

'I'd be piling up old bottles, rusty paint tins, smelly bags of rubbish, noxious weeds, filling huge litter bags. Then I'd be lugging up rotting mattresses, old refrigerators, rusty gutters and iron sheeting, car bonnets and other crap, feeling very anguished about life early on, and not wanting to have a conversation with anyone. I'm sure the old deros who sometimes used to sleep in burrows they'd hollowed under the lantana, drinking their bottles of metho, thought the mad bag lady was madder than they were.

'I kept going. It was a sad waste of a stunning site and it needed rescuing with some love and care. So in my usual obsessive and perfectionist way, I just fixed it up, trying to make this sickly land look beautiful again.

'I was just cleaning up a mess, literally and, I suppose, symbolically too, desperately cleaning up a mess that I could clean up, when we'd all tried so hard but lost the fight to clean up Brett's addiction. I had this urgent mental and emotional need to get some order back into our lives.'

Wendy never asked anyone's permission, 'Because I couldn't bear dealing with red tape and officialdom and getting a negative response. No one's ever tried to stop me, so I didn't stop. Besides, I didn't have any grand plan to put forward. I didn't have any notion that my first patch of garden under the fig tree would keep expanding for the next twenty-three years. And I still haven't stopped.'

At the bottom of those first entry stairs, you'll see a Brett Whiteley carved wooden figure, *Nude,* 1962, mounted on a rusted metal base beside the now-exposed ancient sandstone cliff face. '*Nude* has travelled a long way,' Wendy says fondly. 'Brett made this sculpture in Sigean in the south of France, where we stayed for a long honeymoon in an isolated farmhouse after we married in London that year.'

The first space you walk into resembles an intimate, grassy-floored amphitheatre, with the verdant garden rising on three sides. 'It's virtually a walled garden,' observes Wendy. 'There's a lovely sense of feeling enclosed and secure.'

So many people have told me they experience a surge of rapture when they enter this first friendly space, as if they're being hugged. Indeed it's become a very popular setting for weddings. Late one summer's afternoon I saw a young woman spontaneously dancing alone here, her slender arms up stroking the air, head and body swaying, off in her own reverie.

'No one's ever tried to stop me, so I didn't stop.'

(**WW**)

Discovering the Secret Garden

LEFT To approach the Secret Garden from Sydney Harbour, come up the lower Walker Street stairs until you see the Whiteley house, then turn right.

TOP Approaching the Secret Garden, across the formal lawns of Clark Park, and walking along the top border known as the Mediterranean garden. The main entry is in front of the tower-topped Whiteley house.

BOTTOM The dense foliage marks the edge of the Secret Garden, which now thrives on formerly landfilled dump land. Sydney Harbour gleams beyond, with its iconic bridge.

The grand staircase leading further down into the garden.

(**WW**) 'In creating the garden, we tried to follow the form of the original cliff and landfilled cove as much as we could. We couldn't bring in bulldozers, trucks, or any machinery. We cleared and carried everything by hand. You can see the top part of the original cliff behind Brett's sculpture.

'I wanted the Secret Garden to be a living, painterly environment which invites people in to use it. I didn't want it to be one of those gardens that's just a static picture, to be admired but not used.'

Discovering the Secret Garden

A clump of tall Bangalow palms graces the centre of the grassy space. 'Arkie gave me those Bangalow palms to plant when I first started clearing,' Wendy says softly.

'Arkie was thrilled about the garden. It was a good feeling to have that daughter–mother approval, and to know that I was finished with drugs and not letting her down any more.'

High up on the Bangalows' ringed trunks, depending upon the season, the palms may be sprouting thick hula skirts of creamy yellow fronds smothered with tiny lilac flowers, or ripe, glistening bronze seeds. Rainbow lorikeets flock in for a nectar orgy when the Bangalows are in flower.

Snug against the Bangalows, and looking awkwardly misplaced like an errant teenager, is a Wollemi pine tree, Australia's famous 'dinosaur tree' or 'living fossil'.

When the first Wollemi pine was discovered in 1994 in a rugged canyon in the Blue Mountains west of Sydney, it was heralded as being the equivalent of finding a small dinosaur alive on earth, because it's a survivor from the Age of Dinosaurs. Wendy is fascinated by the pine's prehistoric foliage, with leaves shaped like a stegosaurus's tail and bark like bubbly chocolate.

'This tree was propagated from the seeds of the first-discovered Wollemi pine,' Wendy explains. 'Sotheby's kindly gave it to me, and I planted it here while I was expanding the garden and deciding where I'd move it permanently. But I left it too long and umpteen experts have since told me if you attempt to move a Wollemi pine it will die, as they hate being moved.

'I wanted to risk it, but my gardeners roundly disagreed, and for once,' Wendy adds with a grin, 'I haven't overruled them. So here the living dinosaur stays – even though I'd love a way to move it.'

Wendy planted her first standard grevillea nearby, and liked it so much, she's planted several more throughout the garden. 'It's an Australian native bush, and a clever nursery started grafting them as standards, so you get this stunning sculptural shape of a weeping dome of foliage on top of a slim trunk. I love its feathery leaves and spidery flowers.'

In the lush tiers of foliage surrounding this first garden room, the datura plants display such an exuberant riot of trumpet-shaped ivory, apricot and peach-hued flowers, it seems nature can be more over-the-top than Liberace or Baz Luhrmann. 'Daturas are so easy to propagate; you just break off a strong stick, shove it in the ground, and it grows,' Wendy declares. 'Then the reward; they have the romance and beauty of an Indian miniature.'

(Wendy cheerily insists on retaining the old name 'datura', even though her pendulous variety of angel's trumpet flowers has been renamed *Brugmansia*.)

Groves of orange, lemon, grapefruit and lime trees, again depending on the season, drip with tiny sweet-scented flowers or swelling citrus fruit.

Visitors wishing to linger or picnic in this first setting will find relaxing chairs and tables under umbrellas and shady branches. A large crepe myrtle spreads above the biggest picnic table, and in summer the branches are so thickly festooned in billowing white floral tresses, it's like a blowsy can-can dancer's petticoats. Birds arrive for a nectar degustation feast, sampling all the Secret Garden's floral offerings.

'Arkie was thrilled about the garden. It was a good feeling to have that daughter–mother approval, and to know that I was finished with drugs and not letting her down any more.'

(*WW*)

Discovering the Secret Garden

(**WW**) 'Arkie's Bangalow palms look
so beautiful in flower, and with their
opulent skirts of seed fronds. A man
who comes to collect their seeds says
they are fine examples of Bangalows.'

Ambling beyond the Bangalows, you'll notice the first of several *objets trouvé*s, unearthed while Wendy and her gardeners were cleaning up literally a hundred years' worth of dumped rubbish. In a typical Wendy touch, she has both honoured the history of the site and added some sophisticated whimsy, by mounting antique junk pieces on stone plinths like treasures.

A hand-operated railway points changer, a porcelain bathroom basin, a rusty metal wheelbarrow, a richly rusted tennis court line-marker, an ancient scooter and tricycle. Neighbour Peter Kingston rescued an aged wooden bench seat from Sydney Harbour and painted 'Lavender Bay' on the back. Mind you, a good eye is required to select and mount found objects, otherwise it's just rubbish.

I've often observed the wave of pleasure that fills adults' faces as they recognise these objects; then nostalgia rolls in as they relate some anecdote to each other, or explain the significance to children.

The garden threads into smaller, more intimate enclaves with shady bowers, some racks of found objects like metal watering cans and billies, and small sculptures like a smile-inducing pair of cast iron clogs for two left feet. Here you'll often find young children playing make-believe games and looking for fairies in what children call 'the fairy garden'.

Sometimes Wendy will ask a wide-eyed child, 'Did you find any fairies?' and, if the answer is 'Yes', she'll ask encouragingly, 'Tell me all about it,' genuinely wanting to hear an outpouring of childhood imagination.

If the answer is a disappointed or sulky 'No,' Wendy will respond amiably, 'Well they're probably just sleeping, so next time you come back, you'll find them.'

Strolling along you'll encounter more picnic tables, a wishing well, banana palms and the pungent fragrances of jasmine and various flowering gingers.

Three mulberry trees are pruned into umbrella shapes so you can reach up and pick the plump ripe berries.

'Do any children keep silkworms these days?' Wendy wonders aloud, passing the mulberry trees. 'When I was a kid, we all had an old shoe box full of fresh mulberry leaves and silkworms. We'd watch the white grubs chewing away at the leaves, growing longer and fatter, then they'd start spinning a yellow silk cocoon around their bodies, like their own burial shroud. It was magical to see. We'd start to unravel the raw silk from a cocoon and wind it around an old wooden cotton reel grabbed from our mother's sewing basket, then grow tired of this as it took forever. The box would be shoved away somewhere and forgotten.

'Months later when you remembered it, you discovered that the silkworms inside the cocoons had turned into moths, the moths had eaten their way out of those cocoons, the male and female moths had bonked each other, the females had laid tiny grey eggs all over the inside of the box, and then the moths died. So the eggs were all ready to complete the life cycle of the silkworm again – egg, lava, pupa, adult. For my generation it was an early lesson in metamorphosis. Now I suppose kids just google it on their smartphones. Am I beginning to sound like a grumpy old woman?' she chortles.

*'Did you find any
fairies? Tell me all
about it. Well they're
probably just sleeping,
so next time you
come back, you'll
find them.'*

(**WW**)

TOP LEFT (*WW*) 'These angel's trumpet flowers are commonly called daturas, although the variety I have, where the flowers hang downwards, is now officially named *Brugmansia*. I still call them daturas. The armchair experts will scold me, no doubt, but *Brugmansia* seems an ugly name for such a heavenly flower.'

TOP RIGHT The Wollemi pine growing in front of the Bangalow palms is Australia's famous 'dinosaur tree' or 'living fossil'. This Wollemi was propagated from the seeds of the first Wollemi pine discovered in 1994 in a rugged Blue Mountains canyon, west of Sydney.

BOTTOM (*WW*) 'The Secret Garden can be like entering a magical dreamworld.'

(WW) Most of the apricot-coloured daturas, and some of the white ones, I propagated from cuttings from historic Bronte House, when my friends the Mullers lived there. Daturas put on such a display of flowers all year round. They are really the dominant flowers in the Secret Garden.

TOP A place to sit under a pomegranate tree that Corrado transplanted from his own home garden.

BOTTOM AND OPPOSITE (*WW*) 'I have always gardened visually, putting together leaves and plants of different sizes and shapes, but I felt that there needed to be some colour in amongst all the green. The plum colour of the iresine looks beautiful with the light on it.

'We've propagated masses of iresine to use throughout the garden, and masses of daturas too. Both are common plants, but used to the right effect they look amazing in a garden.'

LEFT Wendy delights in carefully selecting and mounting found objects – *objets trouvés*.

(**WW**) 'Ruben carved the seat for this bicycle so children could sit on it.'

ABOVE (**WW**) 'Little kids are enchanted by the garden. Many go looking for fairies – someone has painted a tiny door here and left a sign beside it saying "Fairies welcome."'

Parents love bringing small children to the Secret Garden.

(**WW**) 'I want changing perspectives, an unfolding array of surprises and delights as you meander through the Secret Garden.'

The top of a staircase leading down from Clark Park into the Secret Garden.

(**WW**) 'Agaves and succulents thrive in this hot dry section.'

'It's amazing how many people have told me they had a childhood secret garden.'

(ww)

Right in the garden's heart is an old thick clump of green and white variegated bamboo, which took on special meaning as soon as Wendy discovered it. This is Wendy's Secret Garden bamboo.

'It was growing here amongst the rubble when I cleared the valley,' she explains. 'It immediately evoked strong memories of my own childhood secret garden in my mother's back garden at Lindfield, and the bamboo clump I used to hide inside to have my own thoughts and daydreams.

'It's amazing how many people have told me they had a childhood secret garden – a place no grown-ups knew about, somewhere they'd go to escape the adult world when they felt misunderstood or lonely; somewhere to feel safe in a secret cubby.' (For more on Wendy's childhood secret garden, see chapter 2.)

The bamboo clump is pruned Japanese-garden style, so you can sit beneath it, appreciating the lower lengths of smooth cane, while the taller leafy ends are supported above on a timber trellis, like a massive umbrella.

Every so often, the hushed atmosphere in the Secret Garden will be broken by the metallic squeal of a train slowly shunting along the railway line, into the siding further towards the Harbour Bridge. The occasional glimpse of a train moving in slow motion behind the trees is another reminder of Lavender Bay's history.

Strolling along, past a deep pit lined with old sandstone blocks, formerly the base of an open stormwater drain (now piped) which tore down the hillside, you'll sight a large bare vertical sandstone rockface.

'We had no idea this impressive rockface was here,' Wendy recalls. 'It was quite exciting uncovering it, and determining that this was the cliff side of the original tidal beach, and Sydney Harbour once lapped in here. So it's a true heritage piece. You can see the core marks where the lower half of the cliff has been blasted back when Railways reconfigured this area.'

Beside the cliff face is a private zone, where the gardeners' two work sheds are located.

At the base is the mulch storage pile. Jay Jay (Jared James), one of the younger gardeners, is expert at the intrepid task of wheeling barrowloads of mulch across to the top of the sheer cliff, then tipping the mulch avalanche to join the pile far below. A timber slab is bolted across the top edge of the cliff, to stop the barrow toppling over with its load, but I admit I wouldn't like to try this task.

Near the bottom of the cliff face, the zigzag path leads up the high side of the valley, zigzagging its way to the top. It's the only path from the bottom to the top of the Secret Garden that has no steps. The gardeners bless the introduction of the zigzag path, as it means they can actually wheel their wheelbarrows full of garden matter up and down this path. Before it was built, it took two strong men to carry each end of a heavy wheelbarrow, as they humped it up and down sets of steps.

The bottom of that staircase, moving into lusher planting.

(**WW**) 'Steps and paths are the bones of the garden, along with rockfaces of cliffs and the largest trees.'

Halfway up, the zigzag path crosses what the gardeners used to call the highway. It's the only step-free path that almost traverses the valley side horizontally, so they can fast-track along it with their wheelbarrows. Both these step-free paths are also welcomed by folk wheeling babies and infants in prams and strollers, along with the more frail visitors who can't cope with steps.

A wondrous maze of other paths and staircases trails all through Wendy's Secret Garden, like a game of snakes and ladders. It adds to the sense of intrigue as you follow an impulse or allow yourself to get happily lost for a while, wondering what you'll savour around the next turn.

At the bottom of the zigzag path, you'll often spot children playing hide-and-seek, a favourite game in the garden as there are so many places to hide. The seekers will be standing, hands covering their eyes, counting aloud to one hundred, then squealing with delight as they race up and down paths and staircases, trying to find the hiders.

The top of the cliff has a large slab of almost flat sandstone. Clenched onto this is a mighty Port Jackson fig tree, its roots clambering into every crevice it can find. Unlike the Moreton Bay fig's broad, glossy, green leaves, the Port Jackson fig has longer, slimmer leaves, a dull olive colour on top with a powdery rusty tone beneath.

'We had to unstrangle this Port Jackson fig, pulling off masses of morning glory vines and other knotted vines with sticky pods,' Wendy remembers. 'You could barely see the tree, and the sandstone cliff was buried under cascades of lantana and privet.'

This part of the garden is shadier, with a massive camphor laurel tree spreading a wide canopy enmeshed with the Port Jackson fig. Wendy admires the natural grandeur of the two giant fig trees standing sentinel at either end of the Secret Garden's main valley, like two markers.

As evening falls, you're likely to see brushtail and ringtail possums in both fig trees, eating the small figs and leaping between the boughs like high-flying trapeze artists performing aerial gymnastics. The brushtail has a black, brushy tail, pink nose, long whiskers and large ears. The ringtail is smaller and shyer, with a long, thin whitish tail which acts as a fifth limb, ideal for tree-swinging.

These innocent-faced nocturnal marsupials shelter and nest in tree hollows and dense vegetation, but unfortunately are also intrepid nesters inside house roofs, and prone to romping on rooftops all night. They also have no table manners, spitting pips and shedding possum poo all over the roofs.

Possums who've made nests in the vines on Wendy's balcony are smartly returned to the garden. A small colony of bats competes with the possums in both fig trees, eating the figs and sleeping in the boughs.

In recent years Wendy's Secret Garden has extended way beyond the Port Jackson fig, east towards Luna Park, as she's cleaned up and beautified the stretch of higher land which dips into a deep gully.

Discovering the Secret Garden

The Port Jackson fig tree clings to the rock cliff that towers above the zigzag path. The zigzag path, the only path from the bottom to the top of the Secret Garden with no steps, enables the gardeners to wheel their wheelbarrows up and down more easily. It is also popular with parents pushing prams.

(**WW**) 'We're going to call this "Ruben's Runway", because he's the gardener who insisted that the zigzag path was badly needed.

'The long, winding path which traverses the top of the valley is now called "Via Corrado", so both my stalwart longtime gardeners have a major pathway named after them.'

'We had no idea this impressive rockface was here. It was quite exciting uncovering it, and determining that this was the cliff side of the original tidal beach, and Sydney Harbour once lapped in here. So it's a true heritage piece.'

(*WW*)

Discovering the Secret Garden

The magnificent camphor laurel.

(*WW*) 'Entering a garden invites you to pause and contemplate the small marvels in nature, and to reflect on your own life.'

(**WW**) 'This isn't a flower garden, as I don't have enough sun. It's more about using foliage, leaf shapes, textures and colours up against each other, like you're painting or sculpting. The pigments I use are plants, leaves, some flowers when I can get them, rocks, mulch, wood, bark. Light and shadow.'

The two bottle trees were originally tiny.

(**JH** to **WW**) 'What will you do when the bottle trees belly out and grow so huge that they block the path?'

(**WW**) (eyes rolling) 'I won't try to move them – to the relief of my gardeners. I'll probably move the path.'

'I treated the garden like a giant painting, structuring, planting, then adding more layers of planting; pruning, editing, moving things around until it pleased my eye.'

(WW)

On the edge of that deep gully, another Wollemi pine is flourishing. 'It was originally in a flowerpot on a nearby resident's balcony, then it outgrew the pot, so the owner brought it over here for us to plant,' Wendy recalls. 'We've acquired quite a few plants this way; when they have outgrown or burst their balcony pots, they've found a new home here.'

On this higher ground you can look across to Luna Park's giant Ferris Wheel and suspended, swaying Pirate Ship. On weekends and school holidays you'll likely hear the echoing, shrill screams of people in the Pirate Ship as it sways back and forth, then does a 360-degree turn. I like one child's internet post, 'Too much fun. I vommed here, twice.'

Returning to the Port Jackson fig, you can weave your way back and forth along the steep, terraced hillside, every path offering multi-perspective vistas to absorb, as you're in such close contact with the planting.

Look up, from directly underneath arching palm fronds and the undersides of teeming canopies of leaves. Peer downwards into the rosette crowns of bird's nest ferns, so huge and luxuriant you could be in a tropical jungle. Or marvel at the crown of a tree fern unfurling new fronds in exquisite 'fiddlehead' forms, as perfect as a violin scroll.

Swivel your eyes sideways and pat the cool bark of bottle trees with swollen trunks like bellies bloated after a feast. Marvel again at the spiral forms of threadlike tendrils, as climbing plants twine themselves around hosts. Scrutinise the quivering, pollen-laden stamens inside hibiscus flowers, awaiting the birds and bees to partake in plants' lovemaking dance of pollination. And squint at the bees getting tipsy, gulping from ravishing quantities of jacaranda and frangipani flowers.

The play of light on all this foliage is always in Wendy's mind; how the effects of light shift and change throughout the day, from the crystal-bright early morning sun, to the low, sloping golden afternoon light.

'I'd never made a real garden before this,' Wendy ventures, 'only a courtyard with pots. I knew nothing about horticulture or Latin names of plants.

'But like Brett, I'm a highly visual person. I do know about colour, shape, texture, design and balance. So I treated the garden like a giant painting, structuring, planting, then adding more layers of planting; pruning, editing, moving things around until it pleased my eye. And letting nature work its own magic – though nature regularly gives you a slap in the face, with invasions of chewing bugs and borers, or possums eating all the new shoots, or mighty storms or droughts – just to remind you who's really boss!

'I do everything visually, so it's big leaves against small leaves, long, strappy leaves against small, feathery leaves, rich plum-coloured leaves swathed and clumped between the greens, greys and silvers.

'I don't ever want a garden that's over-neat, or looks like it's been over-planned by a professional landscape designer. Nothing in straight lines, and certainly no perfectly clipped buxus hedges.'

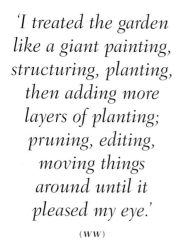

Wendy's eclectic yet harmonious mingling of natives, exotics, palms and fruit trees, with an understorey of ferns, succulents, bromeliads, creepers and matted groundcovers, constantly delights the eye and spirit.

When the numerous varieties of bromeliad are flowering, the surreal display of vivid colours and dazzling shapes in the blooms emerging from the spikey leaf cups rivals a parade of cardinals adorned in full ceremonial regalia. The colour combinations flaunted are fabulously vulgar: shocking pink and electric blue, shrill scarlet and gaudy orange, garish magenta and vermilion.

Over lunch of Corrado's homemade pizzas with Wendy and the gardeners, we wonder if nature gives these Mardi Gras flowers to plainer or dorky-looking spikey plants, like bromeliads and cacti. The gaudy blooms become their siren call to seduce birds and insects needed to fertilise them. Daturas, however, are voted the divas of the horticultural catwalk when it comes to sheer abundance in flamboyant flowering.

The top border of the Secret Garden, where it meets Clark Park, is called the Mediterranean garden. It's filled with lavenders, prostrate rosemary, salvia, echium, plants with smaller, hardier silvery-grey leaves and smaller-petalled heads of blue and lilac flowers, which are more suitable to the drier soil and hotter conditions in this strip. Long trails of nasturtiums creep between the bushes, the yellow, orange and red flowers like licks of flame amidst the groundcover. Thick tresses of blue plumbago tumble wantonly from the top of the Mediterranean garden, over the edge of the valley. Gymea lilies shoot up deep red flowers atop tall stems.

As well as developing its own microclimate, the Secret Garden has transformed itself from near sterility to rampant fertility. Healthy plants and trees now snuggle against each other.

'When we started the soil was shocking,' Wendy recalls. 'There barely was any soil, it was mostly crumbled sandstone rubble and dust. As we brought in masses of good new soil, planted, watered and mulched, the trees and plants grew, the mulch and falling leaves composted and the soil kept improving. Taller trees provided shade so new plants could thrive underneath, plants that struggled in the early years took off, and they all helped each other grow. The soil became sweeter, the air became sweeter, birds and bees arrived in droves; we needed to water and fertilise less. Plants now love growing here, and many self-seed new offspring wherever the seeds scatter. Indeed, everything is now growing so well, the branches are fighting each other to crane up to get the sun, so a major ongoing task now is judicious pruning and thinning.'

'I don't ever want a garden that's over-neat, or looks like it's been over-planned by a professional landscape designer. Nothing in straight lines, and certainly no perfectly clipped buxus hedges.'

(WW)

Throughout the years, Wendy's Secret Garden has harboured many secrets.

One that can be mentioned is the grove of jacarandas planted in memory of Arkie, because jacarandas flower around the time of Arkie's birthday in November. Some years the colour is so intense, it looks as if Brett's been up in the sky with his hands full of giant paintbrushes, sweeping a purple-blue blaze over Lavender Bay.

(**WW**) 'I want people to immerse themselves in my garden, and this part is almost like a rainforest. But I don't want that total rainforest effect, which can feel too sunless and closed-in. I always want shafts of sunlight beaming through the canopy, so I keep pruning to allow this. The play of light on the leaves and trunks is all part of the effect I'm after.'

(WW) 'If you're feeling empty, or in need of replenishment, nature can fill you up. Open your eyes, pause, and let yourself see.'

(**WW**) 'We used weathered sandstone rocks from the landfill to make dry stone walls, which are basically retaining walls to stabilise the steeply sloping site. I like plants to spill over the dry stone walls to soften them, but not to obscure them.'

(**WW**) 'This white bat flower plant has an intriguing flower, like a bat's face with big white floral leaf ears and long curling whiskers. It's quite a rare plant, and very hard to grow. My neighbour Kingo has one in his garden, and gave me one for the Secret Garden. I'd love more.'

LEFT (**WW**) 'I like some pinks, but they must have a strong balance of green. I hate the synthetic-looking pinks in several modern breeds of plants, that look so genetically modified and fed on steroids, they shout out, "fake, bad mistake," like bad facelifts.'

ABOVE A ponytail plant, with its ponytail of long hair-like leaves.

(**WW**) 'If I had more sun in this garden, I could grow more flowers. I'd love to have a blue and white flower garden, mixed together; or an all-white garden like Vita Sackville-West's garden at Sissinghurst Castle in England.

'I love the intensity you can get with different blues. Both Brett and I always felt a special connection to the colour blue. Brett raved about Winsor and Newton's French Ultramarine blue. The agapanthus in the above photo is about as close as you can get to French Ultramarine.'

LEFT (**WW**) 'One of the jacarandas I planted for Arkie.'

OPPOSITE (**WW**) 'When I am working in the garden, I become obsessed. I might intend just to go for a short time, but end up staying till dark, always seeing more that I want to do.'

'... they might lie on the ground, feel the earth against their bodies, open their eyes and really look at a blade of grass, a crawling ant, a fallen leaf, for the first time in their life'

(*WW*)

'I love jacarandas, and Sydney used to be full of them, but councils seem intent on cutting them down in public places as they drop so many flowers on footpaths, make a mess and people might slip on them,' laments Wendy. 'This nanny-state thinking so irritates me. Can't people look where they're putting their feet? I relish the seasonal ritual of falling flowers and leaves, because then you see the naked bark form of the trunks.

'People do go on about flowers in their prime, but I also love watching the graceful process of life ebbing away from a full bloom. Petals drop one by one, leaves slowly shrivel to reveal a smooth sculptural seed pod. Left to dry and burst forth its seeds, it becomes another extension of natural beauty.'

Brett loved jacarandas, and his 1977 oil *The Jacaranda Tree (on Sydney Harbour)* won that year's Wynne Prize. He loved painting frangipanis too, and frangipani trees propagated from many friends' trees are dotted all through the garden.

It brings Wendy pleasure to see the enjoyment so many people gain from spending time in the Secret Garden. She watches harassed office workers at lunchtime, escaping their airconditioned cubes and man-made environments, yearning for moments of peace amid sunshine and greenery. They stride down to the Secret Garden to fill their lungs with fresh air and reset their brains, quietly eating a sandwich under a tree and letting their eyes contemplate nature.

'Or they might lie on the ground, feel the earth against their bodies, open their eyes and really look at a blade of grass, a crawling ant, a fallen leaf, for the first time in their life,' she says 'and be amazed at the detail they discover. It could start a whole new way of seeing and thinking.'

Several visitors have gone home, stimulated to start their own gardens from scratch, or work on their existing gardens with renewed determination.

Wendy understands that many people seek out public gardens as a place for private thoughts or intimate conversations, so she allows for this with numerous secluded nooks.

Lovers stroll dreamily through the garden; others arrive alone to soothe a distressed heart, or just have some time out to savour the peace inside the garden.

Countless people have sent Wendy handwritten notes, saying they entered the Secret Garden feeling stressed, tense, sad, depressed, but left with their humanity restored. Others say they left elated, 'Feeling like I was walking on air'.

CHAPTER 5

The History of the Secret Garden

Brett Whiteley
View from window (detail), circa 1973
Pen, brush and ink, 50.6 cm x 75.6 cm
Brett Whiteley Studio Collection
Photo: AGNSW © Wendy Whiteley

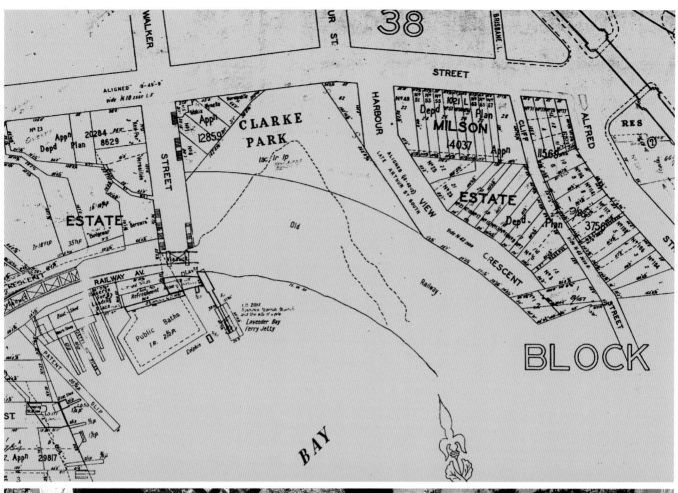

TOP This block plan from the 1930s shows the original tidal shoreline. The area marked with a dotted line was originally a swimming beach. The land was resumed and filled in to make way for the new railway in the early 1890s. Wendy has created the Secret Garden on that disused, landfilled land. The newly created (but misspelt) Clark Park, which adjoins Wendy's Secret Garden, is clearly marked.

BOTTOM An aerial view of the same land, taken in 2015. The Whiteley house is the lowest in the row of houses, far left.

*I*f you stand on the balcony of Wendy Whiteley's house, and gaze east across the Secret Garden, towards the Sydney Harbour Bridge and the Opera House, you can envisage the original shape of Sydney Harbour when the First Fleet arrived in 1788.

The Lavender Bay shoreline of the harbour that greeted Captain Arthur Phillip and his eleven ships after their long voyage from England to settle the colony, was a very different shape from Lavender Bay today.

The evolution of the harbour's changing foreshore unfolds like a detective story, revealed by leafing through hundreds of early maps, council plans and grainy photographs in the Heritage Centre at North Sydney Council's Stanton Library.

In 1788, a sheltered Sydney Harbour tidal beach washed into a deep, V-shaped cove, which sliced inland into Lavender Bay. Tall sandstone rocks edged this cove.

Early maps show that this V-shaped cove lies beneath what is today Wendy's Secret Garden. The cove reaches the Mediterranean garden, the top border where the Secret Garden meets Clark Park. Indeed, the tip of the cove lies several metres further inside Clark Park.

The environmental sacrifice of burying this unspoiled prime harbour cove in order to build a railway line across its mouth would never be allowed today.

Yet the irony is that, if it hadn't been for New South Wales Railways filling in the cove from 1890 to 1893, as well as resuming and reconfiguring the Lavender Bay foreshore, there wouldn't be a Wendy's Secret Garden here today.

———

Aborigines from the Gamaragal clan were living their traditional lifestyle around the bay when European settlers arrived. During Governor Phillip's time, colonists were invited to Aboriginal corroborees. It wasn't long, however, before the traditional culture of the local Indigenous population began to suffer due to the impact of the new settlers.

'Lavender Bay was first known as "Quiberee", the Aboriginal word for the fresh water stream here at the time, which ran into the harbour,' says Wendy. 'The Indigenous folk doubtless regarded it as theirs, and must have wondered what in blazes was happening on their land.'

In the colony's early years, the bay became known as Hulk Bay, after the derelict ship *Phoenix* moored there as a prison for convicts sent from Britain to serve out harsh sentences. At night convicts were locked in leg-irons in cells on the hulk. By day, convict labour gangs built roads and a naval arsenal on Goat Island. They filled casks with fresh water from the stream running into the bay, then rafted the lashed-together casks to ships in the harbour.

'If you let your mind drift back to the First Fleet days, you can almost hear the ghosts of those poor wretches imprisoned in the old hulk on Lavender Bay,' says Wendy. 'Many convicts had only stolen a loaf of bread or a bolt of cloth.'

Lavender Bay became a landing point on the northern side of Sydney Harbour, which was slower to develop and less populated.

'The Indigenous folk doubtless regarded it as theirs, and must have wondered what in blazes was happening on their land.'

(WW)

The History of the Secret Garden

Holtermanns Exp
N.S.Wales Scenery
No 4

Part of the famous Holtermann
panorama of photographs taken in
1875 by Charles Bayliss, from the
top of a 27-metre tower that Bernard
Holtermann specially built above his
Lavender Bay home.

Sydney Opera House now stands
on Bennelong Point, the needle-like
point top centre in this photograph.

Sydney Harbour Bridge now spans
the two points below, virtually above
the bow of the largest boat. The
eastern foreshore of Lavender Bay
is yet to be dramatically altered by
the railway development.

The original Lavender Bay baths, ferry wharf, and McMahons Point, photo-graphed circa 1889, by Henry King.

The popular public baths occupied the cove, before this area was landfilled in 1893 to build the railway. Fred Cavill, swimming teacher and proprietor of the baths, is posed in his best clothes, overlooking his baths.

'People today wrongly assume it was called Lavender Bay after the glorious lavender-blue haze of jacaranda flowers that fills the skies around the bay at the start of summer. Still, it seems destined as the perfect name.'

(WW)

A vast section of the northern foreshore from Kirribilli to Berry Island, had been granted to a handful of men, in individual land grants, and was mostly fenced off with no public access.

William 'Billy' Blue, an enterprising Jamaican-born sailor and ex-convict, in 1817 was granted 80 acres on the western side of Lavender Bay, extending from Blues Point Peninsula across to the centre of the bay. Blue became a ferryman and prospered, building up a fleet of boats.

One of Blue's daughters, Susannah, married George Lavender, a boatswain on the *Phoenix*, and they lived nearby. By the mid-1850s the convict hulk was no longer moored in the bay, so Hulk Bay became known as Lavender Bay, after George Lavender.

'People today wrongly assume it was called Lavender Bay after the glorious lavender-blue haze of jacaranda flowers that fills the skies around the bay at the start of summer,' observes Wendy. 'Still, it seems destined as the perfect name.'

A large stretch of land on the eastern side of Lavender Bay, from Milsons Point to lower Walker Street, was granted to free settler James Milson in 1833. He built an imposing family residence, Brisbane House, on a high point overlooking the bay.

The Milson family enjoyed the beach in the V-shaped cove at the bottom of their ample garden, apparently regarding it as their private property. But by the 1860s, many members of the public, adults and children alike, were also bathing at this beach, which was known colloquially as 'the reserve'. Milson so disapproved of this that he applied for ownership of the foreshore land, down to the low-water mark.

This application was challenged, and the 1860s saw a successful public campaign, which resulted in legislation being passed to make the Lavender Bay beach public property, available for public use and enjoyment. The victory was only short-lived, however, as thirty years later, in 1890, the Lavender Bay beach cove would be lost, resumed and filled in by New South Wales Railways to enable the railway line to proceed in an easy arc along the realigned foreshore.

But much happened in sheltered, picturesque Lavender Bay in the intervening thirty years. The popular harbour beach soon boasted a shark fence to enable safer public bathing. Public swimming baths were erected nearby, along with refreshment rooms. The bay was also home to a bustling collection of boat builders' work yards, boatsheds, a kiln which burnt seashells to obtain lime, a ferry wharf, and private jetties with private bathing enclosures.

Billy Blue's and Milson's land grants were subdivided, and the slower pace of development on the north side of the harbour now quickened. As well as clumps of humble workers' cottages, the foreshore became dotted with fine houses built by wealthy new residents, who planted gracious, English-style gardens. Quiberee, a stone house built for Mathew Charlton, the first mayor of the local borough, still remains on Lavender Crescent, meticulously renovated. Also remaining is Berowra, a handsome stone residence built for a wool broker in 1888 near the bottom of Walker Street steps.

A large slice of this early Sydney history disappeared when the decision was made to extend the railway line serving the growing North Shore population. In what was then regarded as progress, the railway was extended from St Leonards to Milsons Point and by a series of tunnels, viaducts, and by filling in Lavender Bay's beach.

This extended train line ended at the original Milsons Point train, tram and ferry terminal (where Luna Park now stands). Passengers and goods then proceeded across Sydney Harbour by ferry.

Construction of the new railway line required extensive resumption of land along its harbour foreshore route, and numerous buildings were demolished.

Two early grand Lavender Bay residences, Neepsend and Hellespont, were resumed, along with their extensive gardens and waterfront jetties, during the railway development. The two homes, which boasted servants' quarters, coach houses and stables, were converted to boarding houses, and later demolished when this section of surplus railway land became Watt Park. Some tall pines and palms in Watt Park are remnants of their private Victorian gardens. Lavender Bay's rocky outcrop headlands were blasted back, and masses of sandstone landfill tipped into the beach cove.

'Then more stone rubble was dumped around the mouth of the bay, like a raised dam wall, to keep the harbour water back and provide a neatly curving platform for the railway line,' explains Wendy.

'This left a deep, wide, barren valley starting inland from the high clifftop land which became Clark Park, swooping downhill, then veering upwards to the newly raised foreshore bank carrying the railway.

'The valley became an eyesore wasteland and communal illegal dump, and was never used by Railways, who only needed the track running along the reconfigured foreshore. It was this wasteland valley that I cleaned up, and rebirthed into the Secret Garden.'

There's a wonderful photograph, circa 1889, of the swimming teacher Professor Fred Cavill, whose world champion swimmer son, Dick, reputedly invented the 'Australian crawl' overarm stroke in Lavender Bay. Professor Cavill, impressively garbed in his best clothes, is posed sitting on a cliff edge, looking down on his Fred Cavill Baths in that original Lavender Bay beach.

A photograph of the same site post-1893, when the railway was completed, shows a steam train travelling along the new rail line, built on a stark moonscape of rocky landfill and blasted-back sandstone cliffs. Landscaping aesthetics clearly weren't on the agenda.

Indeed, the high section of raw blasted-back cliff face clearly visible in that photograph can now be seen inside Wendy's Secret Garden, with a huge Port Jackson fig tree growing on the top (see photographs on pages 120 and 121).

The late boat builder, Bob Gordon, who arrived in Lavender Bay in 1937, knew its history intimately and was the last boat builder to work there, once remarked, 'The attitude in those

'The valley became an eyesore wasteland and communal illegal dump, and was never used by Railways, who only needed the track running along the reconfigured foreshore.'

(WW)

The History of the Secret Garden

TOP The steam train chugging along the newly built railway line and viaduct, sweeping around the front of newly landfilled Lavender Bay, circa 1905.

The Lavender Bay bathing enclosure then became the local swimming venue, beside the ferry wharf and boat sheds.

MIDDLE Postcard circa 1905 shows the height of the raised railway embankment, resembling a dam wall, running along the reconfigured Lavender Bay.

BOTTOM Sydney Harbour Bridge proudly crossed the harbour in 1932, bringing dramatic change to the original Lavender Bay.

This photograph, circa 1937, shows Luna Park and the Olympic Pool now built on the site of the original Milsons Point train and ferry terminal. Rows of railways sidings lines allow for trains to be stored and cleaned in non-peak hours. The formal lawns and trees of newly planted Clark Park occupy the high ground above the bay.

OPPOSITE TOP Lavender Bay, 2015.

OPPOSITE BOTTOM (WW) 'Lavender Bay wharf today, where Brett used to jump off the edge and swim in the harbour. The old wooden ferry we loved catching from Lavender Bay to Circular Quay no longer runs, but the wharf is still used by private vessels.'

119

View in Lavender Bay.
Kerry, Photo: Sydney.

'*It was an interesting melange of grot, with the rundown buildings and foreshore industries, but you looked out on this utterly glorious harbour, with boats scudding, seagulls circling in the sky and a green fringe of palms and trees.*'

(ww)

The History of the Secret Garden

days was that there were no ecological considerations. If you wanted to push all the rubble into the harbour and put a railway around the foreshore, then you did just that. The contours of the bay were changed forever by the railway.'

Development of Sydney Harbour's northern foreshore suburbs continued apace.

Thomas Walker had been granted 100 acres of land, part of which ran down between Blue's and Milson's land, providing access to the bay. This access strip became known as Lower Walker Street, but the confusingly named 'street' was only ever a long series of steps. Wendy has climbed up and down these steps thousands of times to reach her front door.

When James Milson's grant was subdivided, builder and alderman Henry Green purchased a long, narrow allotment, running down between the east side of Lower Walker Street steps and Clark Park. Green divided this strip into six descending small lots for resale.

On the bottom lot, Number 1 Walker Street, Green built the 1907 Federation house Lochgyle, where Wendy lives today (albeit converted from its original two storeys into four storeys, and wholly renovated in a manner that would dazzle Green). Shopkeeper Abraham Taylor bought Lochgyle in 1908.

The opening of Sydney Harbour Bridge in 1932 brought more dramatic change. Some 500 houses in Milsons Point and North Sydney were demolished to make way for the new bridge approaches and rerouted railway. Cross-harbour travel was revolutionised. The North Shore trains no longer ran around Lavender Bay. Instead, the service was diverted to a new station built at North Sydney and a relocated Milsons Point station, so the line could proceed over the Harbour Bridge. Ferry services across the harbour were substantially reduced.

The railway line around landfilled Lavender Bay, in use for only thirty-nine years, was scaled back to a sidings. 'Trains are shunted in to be stored and cleaned in non-peak periods. They travel in and out very slowly, so it's fairly quiet,' Wendy explains.

The Number 1 Walker Street house had changed hands several times, and been converted into two flats, when the Whiteleys became top-storey tenants in 1969. They bought the property in 1974, soon adding the distinctive Rapunzel's tower staircase to connect the two levels, as there was no interior staircase.

'When we moved into Lavender Bay in late 1969, it was a down-at-heel backwater that barely rated a mention,' Wendy recounts. 'The landed gentry who'd lived around here in earlier years moved away when the inland harbour foreshores west of the Bridge became increasingly industrialised. We had a huge gasworks, a coal loader, an oil refinery and sawmill all nearby, along with numerous boat builders. The eastern side of the harbour, towards the ocean, was regarded as *the* desirable residential area.

'Most of the houses around here were pretty dilapidated, and many were divided into pokey boarding houses with rickety staircases. Plonked among these were dreary blocks of liver-coloured brick flats. It was an interesting mélange of grot, with the rundown buildings and foreshore industries, but you looked out on this utterly glorious harbour, with boats scudding,

That same historic cliff face today in Wendy's Secret Garden. A Port Jackson fig grows on top, and a pile of mulch sits below. The zigzag path runs beside.

seagulls circling in the sky and a green fringe of palms and trees. The entire harbour was bathed in bright blue light and glistening sunshine, which lifted your spirits.'

Wendy recalls the two-storey wooden bathhouse structure in Lavender Bay. 'Brett and Arkie used to swim there when we first moved in. It fell into disrepair and was demolished in 1975, but Brett still dived off the jetty and braved the sharks! We used to catch a wonderful old wooden ferry from Lavender Bay Wharf to Circular Quay and back, then that ferry service stopped. We sometimes hired small, flat-bottomed, putt-putt engine boats with blue and white striped canopies, to potter around the bay.'

Lavender Bay was already well-established as an artists' enclave when the Whiteleys moved in. Wendy elaborates. 'Brett and I knew that Lavender Bay was a treasure trove of early Australian history.' The mixture of foreshore industry, run-down housing, cheap rents and backwater ambience had been attracting artists and writers to Lavender Bay for decades.

'Darling old Lloyd Rees lived a couple of bays north at Northwood, and was still catching ferries and painting his beloved harbour.'

As a teenager, Brett Whiteley so admired Rees' paintings that he traipsed around Lavender Bay and McMahons Point, trying to find the exact spot where Rees had stood to paint.

Indeed, I still have a sketch that Brett Whiteley rapidly drew in my notebook when I was asking him about this, showing where he stood to copy Rees' *The Harbour from McMahons Point (1950)*. A Lloyd Rees Lookout is now signposted off Middle Street, McMahons Point, to mark the exact spot. Roland Wakelin, Rees' great friend, often painted around the area.

In the 1890s, Arthur Streeton painted around Lavender Bay – *Morning Sketch (also known as McMahons Point Ferry)* and *From McMahons Point – Fare One Penny* are two notable works.

In his own artistic homage, the younger Rees had clambered around the foreshore trying to find the exact spot where Streeton had stood, to copy Streeton's admired paintings.

***

When the Whiteleys first rented in Lavender Bay, artist and architect Rollin Schlicht lived downstairs, and artist Peter (Kingo) Kingston moved in next door.

Artist Tim Storrier and his first wife, Sharon, bought the residence three up from the Whiteleys, and lived there with sons Ben and Luke. They planted a jacaranda in the house's narrow raised front garden. The jacaranda is now huge, its roots splitting the sandstone block garden wall. The Storriers no longer live in the house, as both remarried and moved elsewhere. Michael and Margo Johnson then lived around the bay, as did Fred Cress and photographer David Moore. Margaret Olley had lived here in her younger years; so had writer and artist Norman Lindsay. Brett's best friend, sculptor Joel Elenberg, often stayed with the Whiteleys.

'Darling old Lloyd Rees lived a couple of bays north at Northwood, and was still catching ferries and painting his beloved harbour.'

(WW)

The History of the Secret Garden

Ruben painting some pre-loved furniture to place in the Secret Garden near the original harbour cove cliffs. Pre-1893, this was a sandy harbour beach.

From artist's model and muse to amateur film star: Wendy plays the beautiful damsel in *Fanta*, a film take-off of the Phantom, a heroic comic book figure. Artist friends Garry Shead and Peter Kingston made several experimental films in the mid-seventies.

(**WW**) 'It was great fun, we improvised most of it on the spot. I'm wearing a knitted cloche hat – the start of my cloche hat era. I loved wearing them pulled low to frame my face.'

'Kingo and I at the time were obsessed with Phantom comics; we loved those early, stilted, primitive drawings of the masked hero.'

(*GARRY SHEAD*)

John Firth-Smith and Ian van Wieringen lived and painted in an old boathouse on Lavender Bay. Firth-Smith then bought a dilapidated Edwardian waterfront house which had been divided into flats, and artist friends Bob Jacks and Garry Shead moved in. Firth-Smith always had some sort of sailing boat, and halcyon, bohemian times were enjoyed in those early years with night-sailing and parties. Shead rented the shop at the top of the Walker Street steps and ran it as a delicatessen to support his painting and experimental films.

Chez Whiteley saw regular gatherings of these artists living nearby, with Wendy a stylish hostess and inventive cook. Robert Hughes, art critic, was a regular visitor when he was in Sydney. Tim Storrier recalls many raucous parties, 'When Brett would turn the music up so many decibels you couldn't hear yourself think. Brett was a natural comic – he could be so funny – and a brilliant mimic. I was always the younger artist admirer, very impressed with his work.' Brett fondly called Storrier 'Stotsie', and Storrier called Brett 'Brer', as in Brer Rabbit.

Garry Shead had told me an anecdote about Tim Storrier hurling an antique brass butler's bell over the balcony at a Whiteley party, so I ask Tim, and he recalls it with mirth. 'Lady Mary Fairfax had given John Olsen a present – an antique brass turtle – and when you hit its head, a bell rang. It was for summonsing the butler or the servants.

'Olsen was rather dismissive of this silly, expensive object, so we took it along to a party at the Whiteleys.' Brett was intrigued with it, and kept hitting the turtle's head and making the bell ring. Then Garry Shead got fed up with Brett ringing this absurd thing and urged me, "For heaven's sake, get rid of it."

'So I threw the turtle as hard as I could over the balcony, into what is now Wendy's Secret Garden, but back then was a forest of lantana. Next morning, Brett said to me, "Listen mate, you'd better go and find the turtle and give it back to Olsen".

'I thought it would be impossible, but I pushed my way into the horrible maze of lantana, and by some fluke I found it almost immediately. I have no idea what's happened to that ridiculous turtle since.'

In the seventies, Garry Shead was rounding up local artist friends to help make his experimental films. Several of Shead's films used locations around Lavender Bay, including the fabled defunct railway line. Back then it was unfenced and easy to clamber onto.

In 1973, Shead directed and edited a ten minute, black and white 16-millimetre film, based on the comic strip hero the Phantom, starring Peter Kingston as Phantom, Wendy Whiteley as the beautiful damsel in distress, and Brett in a cameo role as the getaway driver.

'We called the film *Fanta*, because of copyright issues with *The Phantom*,' Shead chuckles. 'Kingo and I at the time were obsessed with Phantom comics; we loved those early stilted primitive drawings of the masked hero.

'We shot the entire film at Lavender Bay, using the old railway line, jumping off the viaducts, racing up the Walker Street steps, and catching the small ferry which used to run from Lavender Bay wharf.'

Four stills from Garry Shead's experimental film *Fanta* illustrate the storyline in the text below.

Fanta's storyline: A shy young man (played by Peter Kingston) boards the ferry, finds a seat and takes a Phantom comic from his bag. He side-glances a beautiful young damsel (Wendy Whiteley), then lowers his eyes back to his comic.

He drifts into a dream … he becomes the Phantom. Suddenly he's in tights, cape and mask, fighting off criminals and thugs who are attacking the damsel. But the thugs overcome Phantom and tie him to the railway line. Phantom struggles to escape before a train comes and crushes him.

Just in time, the beautiful damsel runs along the railway line, unties Phantom and rescues him. Phantom leaps off the viaduct, confronts the criminals, and punches down a tall thug (played by John Firth-Smith). Brett Whiteley whizzes up, driving his Mini Moke, the heroic Phantom leaps into the open car, and they speed away.

At this moment, the shy passenger snaps out of his dream. He's still on the ferry, which is about to dock. He looks despondent, as he realises he hasn't even managed to make eye contact with the beautiful damsel. They both get up and leave separately; she walks out of his dream. But the real Phantom is riding on the ferry, and is the last to disembark.

So many memories of yesteryear tumble out when Wendy, Shead and Kingston watch this old black and white film today. 'It's like a window into another time,' says Shead, 'a depiction of an earlier lost world.'

Shead has a more melancholy memory, of a 1973 trip with Brett in his Mini Moke to the New South Wales south coast town of Thirroul. D.H. Lawrence lived there in a clifftop house, Wyewurk, in 1922, while he wrote the book *Kangaroo*.

'I was obsessed with Lawrence,' says Shead, 'and Brett suggested we paint a joint diptych on the same theme: what Lawrence saw as he walked on the beach, thinking about writing *Kangaroo*.

'After a big whisky-drinking night in the Thirroul pub, we talked our way into the house next door to Wyewurk and went to opposite ends of the garden to do our paintings. They came together surprisingly well. I painted a wild landscape of the cliff and sea, while Brett painted a whirling picture of the inside of Lawrence's mind. He added a swirl across mine to link the pictures up, but I wasn't allowed to touch his!

'Brett was adamant that Patrick White have first option to buy it; no one else was allowed to see it. The paintings were hinged, like a book, and tied with a bow. Patrick arrived, the paintings were ceremoniously revealed, but Patrick was unimpressed. Brett was rather pissed off.'

Shead remembers Brett stopping on the roadside on the way back from Thirroul, and romantically picking a big bunch of wildflowers to take home to Wendy.

It was at Thirroul, nineteen years later, that Brett's life ended.

Peter Kingston's 1973 etching of domestic activity inside the Whiteley home on a summer weekend afternoon.

(**WW**) 'We all added something to the picture, then Brett came up with the title *Has Debbie Reynolds Sold her Bus Tickets Yet?* I don't know why he chose that quirky title.'

OPPOSITE Luna Park and Sydney Harbour Bridge.

(**WW**) 'Brett and I both went to Luna Park as kids. Luna Park, Just For Fun. We had a lot of fun on the thrills-and-spills rides, and we took Arkie there too.'

'Brett and I used to swim off the wharf and risk the sharks and stingrays. Brett was always willing to take risks. Wendy would run down to the wharf in her nightie early in the morning to buy fresh fish from Carmello, the Italian fisherman.'

(PETER KINGSTON)

Peter Kingston has been the Whiteleys' neighbour and friend since 1972. He studied architecture at the University of New South Wales, but his passion for art soon dominated his career. A sensitive, restless, compassionate man, Kingston is devoted to preserving the heritage and nostalgic charm of Sydney Harbour, including the original Luna Park rides and artworks, and his paintings often fondly depict harbour life. He laments the gentrification of Lavender Bay, the loss of crusty old characters and skilled artisans, and the invasion of plastic-hulled boats replacing the wooden boats that once swung on moorings in the bay.

'When I arrived here we had fifteen boatsheds in Lavender Bay; a ketch or some other interesting boat was always being serviced at Neptune Engineering, and Bob Gordon was building custom-made boats under the viaduct.

'Brett and I used to swim off the wharf and risk the sharks and stingrays. Brett was always willing to take risks. Wendy would run down to the wharf in her nightie early in the morning to buy fresh fish from Carmello, the Italian fisherman. Carmello was agog serving her!'

In 1973, Kingston made an etching, showing the typical domestic activity inside the Whiteley household on a summer's afternoon. Wendy and her friend Diana Darling are mending a mosquito net. Brett is wearing his "Oysters Think" T-shirt and putting on a record. Another longtime friend, Joanna Collard, is standing in the kitchen,' Kingston explains.

'Then everyone present added something to my etching. Brett did the profile of Joel Elenberg at the foot of the Buddha, and Arkie added a halo on top of the Buddha. Brett made up the title, *Has Debbie Reynolds Sold Her Bus Tickets Yet?*, and I wrote that on the etching.'

When a group of homeless folk transformed a railway viaduct arch near the bottom of Walker Street steps into a shelter, complete with armchairs, settee and coffee table, it inspired another touching Kingston drawing, *Domestic Scene, 1993*.

In the seventies Kingston worked at Luna Park with fellow artists Martin Sharp and Garry Shead, restoring the fairground's original artwork. Luna Park was then enjoying its heyday, with the giant rollercoaster, river caves and Coney Island rides full of customers.

Luna Park had opened in 1935, on the site of the workshops of Dorman Long and Company, which built the Harbour Bridge. Arthur 'Art' Barton, born in 1887, was the artist employed at Luna Park from when it opened until 1970, when he retired due to failing eyesight. Barton designed the happy-faced clown entrance that became the iconic image of Luna Park, used as the model for all subsequent Luna Park faces. Barton died in 1974, and Art Barton Park, beside Luna Park, was opened in 2007 in his memory.

In 2002 Kingston made a series of small bronze statues, commemorating his childhood storybook and comics heroes. The statues are mounted along the boardwalk from Lavender Bay

to Luna Park, in a section known as the Comic Walk. You can spot Bib and Bub, Ginger Meggs, Boofhead, the Magic Pudding, Blinky Bill, Felix the Cat and more.

From his house next door to the Whiteley house, Kingston has watched Wendy's Secret Garden grow from its inception. 'The land was a very depressing sight, with a big open drain, before Wendy started,' he recalls. 'The only thing I liked were the little blue-tailed wrens that lived beneath the undergrowth. It's extremely commendable what Wendy has done here; I really love the garden.'

Like most neighbours, Wendy and Kingston have had their squabbles, particularly over the appropriate variety of tree to plant. 'Kingo wants angophoras in a place where I prefer jacarandas,' huffs Wendy.

Early on, Kingston planted three grevilleas on the edge of the Secret Garden near his balcony, plus a dozen rainforest trees. 'Then I stepped sideways and concentrated on the boardwalk,' he notes diplomatically.

For many years Kingston would try to engage then Prime Minister John Howard on his morning walk. The PM strode from Kirribilli House on a foreshore circuit, coming up the Walker Street steps then along the top of the Secret Garden and through Clark Park, 'within spitting distance' of the neighbouring Whiteley and Kingston balconies. Kingston would be out at dawn, marking chalk drawings on the bitumen path, be it 'Save the Dugong', or 'Save the Walsh Bay wharves', hoping the visual message might imprint itself on the Prime Ministerial brain.

'Julia Gillard and Kevin Rudd have come striding by too. Quentin Bryce did a tour of the garden when she was Governor-General,' he says, 'and had tea at Wendy's house. One day Deborra-Lee Furness, Hugh Jackman's wife, was panting up the Walker Street steps looking hot and bothered. She stopped me, looking exasperated, and asked, "Where is Wendy's Secret Garden?"

'There was no signpost, so people could get a bit confused trying to find the entrance.'

Wendy adds that Deborra-Lee was a good friend of Arkie's, the two having met in the acting world. 'Deborra-Lee came back to visit the garden with Hugh and their two kids, and they signed one of our early visitors' books.'

The legendary Australian writer Henry Lawson (1867–1922) resided in numerous dwellings near Lavender Bay between 1885 and 1922, catching the ferry across the harbour to the offices of *The Bulletin*, where he worked.

Lawson is best known as a great Australian poet of the bush, but he also wrote with real affection about the local folk he yarned with in Lavender Bay: in the street, on the ferry and in the pub. There are stories of Lawson staggering home from the pub, quoting poetry aloud after a glass too many. Lawson cast a thoughtful eye on all classes of people, from the well-to-do to urchins in rags racing homemade billycarts down footpaths.

After the railway line went in and Lawson could see trains running along the line below where he lived, he wrote 'Above Lavender Bay'. The poem describes his image of toy trains and

a toy station, the beauty of rich dark greenery, gullies of waratahs, and 'a moonlight night in middle-age / That makes one feel like a child'.

Lawson's daughter, Bertha, was born in North Sydney in 1900. In the late sixties, Bertha unveiled the Henry Lawson Memorial Seat in Blues Point Road, near William Street, saying it was a place where people could pause and remember, laze and dream, or just rest and be human.

Bertha's thoughts apply so perfectly to those who go and sit in Wendy's Secret Garden.

Wendy observes, 'You can easily imagine that you're back in an earlier century when you are in the calm seclusion of the Secret Garden. You can look up at the extreme contrast of Kirribilli's wall of highrise buildings, or gaze across to the towering mass of Sydney CBD skyscrapers. At night the city glows, like you're staring at another planet.'

It is a historic coincidence that an uneasy fate now hovers over the future of Wendy's Secret Garden, which is built on the very same site where a beautiful natural beach once loved by the public was previously destroyed.

In 1890 the Lavender Bay beach was lost forever, resumed and filled in by New South Wales Railways. Just one hundred years later, Wendy Whiteley began building her Secret Garden on top of that buried public beach.

There's now a widespread public desire, fuelled by the hundreds of thousands of people who've visited, for the land Wendy's Secret Garden occupies to be permanently legislated public land, for public use and enjoyment. Visitors from all over Australia, indeed all over the world, write passionate pleas in Wendy's Secret Garden visitors' books, asking the New South Wales Government to protect the Secret Garden and ensure its future.

It would be a fitting historic redemption if the New South Wales Government could make this happen, especially now that the buried beach has been awakened from its long slumber, and transformed into a glorious, artistic garden.

This resurrection has cost the Australian and New South Wales Governments nothing. Wendy Whiteley has done it magnificently for them, and Wendy and her gardeners continue to enhance the greatly loved garden for the public. It's her gift, one that she fervently hopes will be preserved, not destroyed.

Great public gardens enhance the identity of an area, and the Secret Garden is now another strong strand enhancing the identity of Lavender Bay.

'You can easily imagine that you're back in an earlier century when you are in the calm seclusion of the Secret Garden.'

(WW)

The Gardeners

(WW) 'Corrado is my favourite Sicilian. Sicilians have great knowledge of the earth, and Corrado is a natural gardener.'

(*CORRADO*) 'Yes, I can have my ideas, but Wendy has to like them! Or else we have a big debate.'

T he way Wendy recalls it, Corrado serendipitously happened to be strolling by on the day she literally reached tipping point.

'I was endeavouring to clear a dense mound of feral brambles and tangled vines below the big Moreton Bay fig tree,' she begins, 'when I fell off a steep rock cliff. I kept sliding down, being ripped by thorns, then I landed in broken glass and rat-infested rubbish.'

Crawling her way back up into the sunlight, Wendy grittily strengthened her resolve that this was not going to defeat her. But she did admit to herself that the time had come when she needed help. She could no longer go on clearing up this entombed valley on her own.

At that moment, a tall, muscular, good-looking Italian, Corrado Camuglia, ambled along the path above the Moreton Bay fig, whistling. Corrado has the lungs of an opera singer and likes to whistle songs when he's in a good mood, and he's mostly in a good mood.

He'd been helping a mate lay bathroom tiles in Berowra, the historic house nearby.

'I looked down and saw a lady struggling in the big green mess,' Corrado relates, with his mellifluous, pronounced Italian accent. 'I like to talk to girls, so I stop and call out to her, "Eh! You need a hand down there?"'

'Yes I do!' Wendy cried in response, waving at the stranger.

Corrado trod confidently down the slope towards her, and Wendy decided she liked the young man's open manner and honest face. 'How'd you like to work for me here, cleaning up this mess?' she proposed.

'I don't mind; I can start on Saturday,' Corrado responded.

'Do you have a truck? I need someone with a truck to start carting this rubbish to the tip,' Wendy added.

'Yes, I have a big ute,' Corrado replied. And thus began the long, fond connection and ongoing 'Use your eyes' tutelage between Wendy and Corrado, the first long-term gardener she hired to work beside her making the Secret Garden.

That was early 1996. Corrado soon became so devoted to the Secret Garden and the mysterious, inwardly driven woman he still defers to as 'She's the Boss', that he began to work for her two, three, four, then six days a week.

'I had no idea she was Wendy Whiteley, widow of the famous artist Brett Whiteley,' Corrado admits. 'Those names didn't mean anything to me, or to my wife, Enza. I was a labourer and at night I ran a pizzeria. I didn't know that she did not own the land. I just thought, well that's the lady's house, so we clean up the land in front of her place. She didn't want to talk much in those early years, so I never asked questions. I just did my job.' Corrado gives one of his familiar easygoing shrugs. 'She just tells me, "Use your eyes!"'

Around the same time, Mrs Keny Gardiol had begun part-time work as a housekeeper for Wendy. Born in Chile, the quiet, slim, modest Keny, with her long, blonde hair and perfect features, also had no idea this was the house of the famous Brett Whiteley, but she sensed that the lady who hired her was bearing a great sadness.

'I looked down and saw a lady struggling in the big green mess. I like to talk to girls, so I stop and call out to her, "Eh! You need a hand down there?"'

(*CORRADO*)

Keny's husband, Ruben, was on a lengthy visit to his Uruguay homeland when he received a letter from Keny about her new job. Ruben, a house painter, knew about the Whiteleys and wrote back informing Keny who Wendy was, hoping she wouldn't be worried that she was working for a celebrity.

'My wife Keny is a bit of a worrier, as well as being very strong-minded,' Ruben says lovingly, 'but luckily Wendy and Keny were already getting on well, so Keny decided to stay.'

Two years on, Ruben was doing some house painting for Wendy, when he mentioned he'd had enough of house painting. Wendy asked Ruben if he'd like to work in the garden.

She also offered Corrado extra work there. He was uncertain. 'I say to Ruben, "This lady stays at home all the time, she doesn't go out to a job; she just works all the time in the garden. How's she gonna be able to pay us?"'

Ruben, who has the same quiet modesty as his wife, Keny, and the manner of an old-fashioned, courtly gentleman, replied cautiously, 'She's in the art world and I think it will be all right'.

Some twenty years on, Corrado, Ruben, Keny, and a new, younger gardener, Jay Jay, are sitting around the table in the gardeners' room in the ground level of Wendy's house, as the early recollections tumble out during their lunch break.

'We're all still here,' Corrado says affectionately. 'We're like family now. And like any family, we all have our moments, and Wendy has her moments; but we adapt to each other, we respect each other.' He adds with a genial smile, 'Only, She's the Boss; Wendy is always the Boss.'

The garden has clearly become an ingrained part of all their identities, and I'm curious about how they remember Wendy from those early years, working beside her daily. Did she seem sad, did she ever share her grief?

Corrado shakes his head. 'Wendy is the way she is. Wendy has always been a very strong woman. She kept those feelings inside, private. She never poured her sorrows onto us. For me, the biggest thing was, Wendy was always very motivated. And she wanted to do things *her way*.

'Arkie was living here sometimes when we first started, and she was such a nice young woman. Arkie loved life, she loved art, theatre, travelling, shopping, always busy-busy. But Wendy loved being in the garden most of all. She'd start working alongside us at 7 a.m. and when we'd go home at 4 p.m. Wendy was still working in the garden till it was so dark you couldn't see. Wendy has such determination, she's such a perfectionist, she just has to stay on finishing up this bit properly. You couldn't stop her.'

Did Wendy ever discuss a big plan for the garden, a grand vision?

'No, never,' Corrado replies. It just happened metre by metre.'

Ruben adds, 'Wendy didn't ever talk like that. She was just clearing up and seeing what was underneath. It was a challenge and we all enjoyed it. I thought it would be a job for just a year, then Wendy goes, "What if we clear that bit down there?" So every year we grab another 50 metres of horrible land, and fix it up so it becomes beautiful.

'We're all still here. We're like family now. And like any family, we all have our moments, and Wendy has her moments.'

(CORRADO)

The Gardeners

Corrado, Wendy, Luke and Ruben.

(*WW*) 'A good garden needs good gardeners. Garden with all your instincts, put your heart and soul into it, and you will be rewarded.'

(**WW**) 'Ruben is from Uruguay. He loves being a gardener. He is absolutely meticulous about whatever he does. He and Corrado are both treasures – but they did have to sort out who did what.

'At the end of the day, they both know that I am the garden designer. I constantly tell them to use their eyes, and mostly they do.'

'I felt an overwhelming desire to do something positive. Doing something creative, right here, was the most freeing thing I could do.'

(WW)

'At the end of each day we'd be sweating, tired, covered in dirt, scratches, insect bites, but we'd stand up the top and look down into the garden. It was so satisfying, and quite exciting too. Previously that land was like a big, sickly body, covered in ugly sores; but now, gradually, it was becoming healthy with new soil, new plants, trees and flowers. New birds started to fly in that we'd never seen before. It felt so good; the garden looked happy and we were happy.'

Ruben and wife Keny sometimes shared their thoughts about what was driving Wendy to do this. Ruben says, 'I always put it down to – well, she likes to beautify the area, she's got the desire and the funds to do it, so that's good for everyone. She was sick of looking at that wasted land, and people kept dumping more layers of rubbish there. Shocking amounts of stuff, rusty corrugated iron, old stoves, old car engines, sump oil, smelly contaminated matter. Lantana would grow over it, then another layer of rubbish was dumped – bottles and rotting mattresses – and weeds grew on top. Corrado and I both own utility trucks, and every day we'd both take a big load of rubbish to the tip on our way home.'

For a period after Brett died, Wendy admits that she did think seriously about moving away from Lavender Bay and changing her name. Well-meaning friends advised her to sell the house, and start again.

'You don't really start again,' she reflects. 'Things change, but you just pick up your bundles and carry on. I decided that I didn't need to reinvent myself further. I'd already reinvented myself from being a drug addict living in unravelling chaos, to a non-drug addict taking back control of my life. I was still like a child learning to walk on steady legs, when Brett's death knocked me flat again. I needed to stay here, because I loved Lavender Bay and Arkie loved this place, and I wanted the family home to be here for her.

'I felt an overwhelming desire to do something positive,' she stresses. 'Doing something creative, right here, was the most freeing thing I could do.

'I suppose I could have started writing a biography or taken up painting again, but that was all too interconnected with going backwards. Making a garden was leaping forwards. Arkie loved seeing the garden evolving, so it was a precious bond that we shared.'

Ruben was particularly fond of Arkie. 'I got to know her earlier, when I was painting the house of Wendy's mother, Mrs Daphne McKenzie. Arkie was living in London and, when she came back home to visit, she'd pop in to see her grandmother. She'd bring me tea and biscuits and stay on to chat. Such a charming young woman, and always so genuinely interested in what everyone else was doing, and asking after our families.

'When I started working in Wendy's garden, Arkie had moved to Palm Beach and had a garden of her own, but she was always visiting Wendy and wanting to see what we were all doing in the garden here. Arkie cared so much about Wendy, they were very close.'

Arkie was holidaying in Bali when she rang Wendy to say she was feeling very sick. Wendy, thinking it was some stomach bug, suggested that Arkie fly back to Sydney and see her doctor. Tests and a specialist's appointment followed.

The Gardeners

TOP (*WW*) 'An early stage of clearing, towards the Walker Street steps.'

MIDDLE (*WW*) 'There was so much undergrowth and rubbish to clear, we made gigantic piles of waste. These bags are full of old cans and bottles and junk. We lugged it all up by hand, then Corrado took it to the tip in his ute.'

BOTTOM (*WW*) 'Arkie's Bangalow palms, just planted, and a standard grevillea in a circle of stones.'

The Gardeners

'Doing something physically demanding also helps, and I soon found that gardening lets me lose myself at those times when I need to lose myself.'

(**ww**)

In September 2001, Arkie arrived at Wendy's house, ashen-faced, bearing X-rays and the specialist's diagnosis of highly aggressive adrenal gland cancer.

'It was nothing but bad news after that,' says Wendy, a mother's sorrow filling her face. 'We tried everything in the next three months, and right until the day she died we couldn't believe this was happening; we kept hoping for the miracle cure. But my daughter was gone, only thirty-seven years old. Beautiful little Ark left us.'

A tenderness enters Wendy's voice when she speaks about Arkie, and she gets a wistful expression in her eyes. You wonder about the inner sadness that will remain part of her forever.

After the funeral, Wendy scattered Arkie's ashes in the Secret Garden, near Brett's ashes. Standing in the garden that night, Wendy had never felt so alone.

Grief-wracked as she was, Wendy was determined not to feel pity for herself. She heaved herself back into the garden, Ruben and Corrado working beside her and watching over her protectively, all grieving heavily as they toiled. No one spoke very much, but their silence spoke volumes.

Labouring beside these good-hearted, honest men couldn't have been a more complete contrast to Wendy's previous role as art superstar's muse and goddess of the art world's opening nights, but I've often thought it was probably her salvation.

Ruben says, 'Wendy can be very tough on herself, the way she contains things inside, but that's her way. You'll never see self-pity. Indeed, she becomes impatient with others who display self-pity.'

Looking back at that time, Wendy today observes, 'You can go both ways with grief. I could have given up, and slid into an abyss of depression, or become suicidal, or gone back on drugs. But I'd already rehearsed death, I'd nearly died enough times down that drug path, so I wasn't going back there. I was especially wary of becoming embittered, or playing the victim.'

First up, know thyself, and Wendy knew herself well enough to reason, 'In order to stay sane, civil and intelligent, I need to be occupied doing something positive, rather than sitting around staring at my navel and feeling depressed about life's slings and arrows, or depressed about growing old.

'Doing something physically demanding also helps, and I soon found that gardening lets me lose myself, at those times when I need to lose myself. Many people discover the gift that gardening gives you back, and it can be quite therapeutic in this way. It's certainly a lot healthier than many other options.'

Corrado observes, 'Right from the start, I could see that Wendy was trying to forget. Even now, for Wendy it's still the best way to forget. If something is not going right for her, she's angry, sad or if she wants to forget something, straight into the garden she goes and starts working hard. She won't come back to the house for lunch, phone calls, nothing. Wendy tells me that she forgets about the world and focuses on that piece of garden and those plants.'

The same view, fifteen years later.

(**WW**) 'We waited a few years to build the first main staircase leading into the Secret Garden. The Bangalows have now galloped in size, as has the Moreton Bay fig.'

Wendy had no previous gardening experience, other than arranging pots on a concrete rooftop in New York's Chelsea Hotel, and the odd courtyard.

'My mother, Dassy McKenzie, was a keen gardener, though I admit that as a kid I didn't take much notice,' she reminisces. 'We had a nice garden on a big, suburban block in Lindfield, and it was mainly my mother who did the gardening. I think it was very important for women of my mother's era to have a garden, because society was still entrenched in the traditional view that the man was head of the household. The garden let housewives have their own domain.

'They could gain a sense of personal pride and achievement from making an admired garden. It was a release from the tedium of housework. Men often looked after the vegetable patch; it was their territory, the solid stuff.'

Wendy had grown up knowing only typical Sydney North Shore suburban gardens. At that time, front gardens were showplaces, neat and pretty as a lace handkerchief, with flower borders along the front fence and driveway, then azaleas and camellias against the side fence. A circle of poppies and dahlias might be embroidered into the clipped front lawn, along with a specimen tree like a silver birch or blue spruce. Back gardens were a less glamorous afterthought, called 'backyards', with a vegetable patch, chook pen, washing line, shed, incinerator, maybe a cubby house or swing. Choko and passionfruit vines grew over the back fence.

The era of front and back designer garden makeovers, paved entertaining areas around designer pools and glamour barbecues, mass-planting in rows and drifts of monotype species, was yet to arrive.

Neither Corrado nor Ruben was a professional gardener, and both had only a limited experience of gardening whilst growing up.

Corrado's father was a gardener in Sicily. 'I used to help him sometimes as a kid, but it was mainly in citrus orchards,' Corrado recalls. 'In 1974, aged fifteen, I came to Australia with my cousin. I started working with a bricklayer, then a plumber. I'm a handyman, so I can build sheds, lay concrete, tiles. I can also cook, so I became a partner in a pizzeria, and I knew a bit about gardening.'

Ruben was born in Uruguay, a descendant of French migrants, and his large family was mostly involved in farming: dairy, wheat, vineyards and citrus orchards. 'I grew up on a farm so I know about growing crops, cutting timber, fixing machines and tools and being resourceful,' he explains.

In 1978, aged twenty-five, Ruben migrated to Australia, where he met and wed Keny, who'd arrived four years earlier from Chile. In Sydney, Ruben started working as a house painter.

What Wendy, Corrado and Ruben all did share was an immediate connection with nature dating back to their earliest days. That childhood absorption in nature was deeply ingrained.

Corrado proclaims, 'But I tell you – we all learned a lot more by making the Secret Garden. Wendy, Ruben and I, we all increased our knowledge about gardening here, on the job. We are all now much better gardeners!'

'I think it was very important for women of my mother's era to have a garden, because society was still entrenched in the traditional view that the man was head of the household. The garden let housewives have their own domain.'

(**WW**)

The Gardeners

141

ABOVE (*WW*) 'Arkie's Bangalows are so happy here that they have self-seeded four or five new ones.'

OPPOSITE (*WW*) 'Daturas are definitely the flower divas of the Secret Garden, flaunting their deliciously blowsy displays all year round. I find them staggeringly beautiful, especially after the rain, when they bloom with even more exuberance. This isn't a flower garden, as there isn't enough sun, but I've dotted daturas throughout the garden and some of them are always flowering.'

TOP (*WW*) 'Our early attempts at stabilising the site, building pockets with rocks, then filling them with new soil I always had to buy. Endless truckloads of good soil have been delivered, then carried down in wheelbarrows and buckets to go into this garden, so it could start growing.'

MIDDLE (*WW*) 'We made retaining walls using rocks and stone rubble that we uncovered in the landfill. We got much better at building rock walls the more we did them.'

BOTTOM (*WW*) 'The beginning of the stairs down from Clark Park. It was my idea to use branches as handrails for the stairs. We looked for branches with the nicest forms, from trees on site, but now we have to bring them in from outside, as they need replacing regularly. We now use hardwood for the posts, as bush branches tend not to last very long.'

'We were sliding down the hill as we struggled to save the terraces from collapsing down the hill. What a sight we were, smothered in mud!'

(*WW*)

The Gardeners

At first they were mainly just clearing, then stabilising the exposed ground, via a series of terraces constructed by reusing rocks from amidst the rubble. Pockets of new, fertile soil and mulch were added on top of the clay and sand, to prepare the terraces for planting.

'There was a jungle of *Monstera deliciosa* growing wild near the Moreton Bay fig,' Wendy relates, 'so we transplanted a lot of this into the initial terraces, trying to get something growing and holding down the soil. It's commonly called "the fruit salad plant" because of the taste of its cucumber-shaped fruit. I'm not overly fond of this plant, but it proved a robust grower in poor soil, and its root system and big shady leaves proved helpful in the first stages of the garden.

'Someone gave us a load of unwanted clivias and agapanthus from their garden, so we planted these too. Soon they were multiplying, giving us a seasonal blaze of orange and blue flowers.

'Then the rains poured down and torrents of water gushed down the slope from the park above, so our first attempts at terracing collapsed. We were sliding down the hill as we struggled to save the terraces from collapsing. What a sight we were, smothered in mud! So we had to get savvier and develop amateur engineering skills to put in stormwater drains, and build stronger terrace walls,' Wendy says.

'I have a great engineer forebear to live up to – C. Y. O'Connor, who built the famous 600-kilometre pipeline from Perth to Kalgoorlie, to pump water uphill. I like to think I've inherited some of his engineering skills.

'The inland side of the valley is so steep, and in those early years we'd spend all day working with our bodies at extreme angles, which was probably very good for our leg muscles,' Wendy recounts, grinning.

They uncovered a pile of old railway sleepers, so used these to make terraces, staking the heavy timber sleepers securely into place with lengths of angle iron. 'Later on we had to heave all the bottom sleepers out, as they rotted in the damp. We learned to place a row of drainage stones beneath the lowest sleeper – forever learning …' she adds. 'It was like winning a battle, when we finally stabilised and terraced that steep side of the valley.'

Right from the start, Wendy would repeat her mantra, 'Use your eyes', when directing where terraces and paths should go, and where shrubs and trees should be planted. She'd hold her hands up to her own eyes and make a frame, to study the visual composition. Everything had to be both aesthetic and practical. Ruben and Corrado nod.

As a rank amateur gardener, Wendy relied on her intuitive ability to know what works visually, along with her usual adventurous, romantic approach.

'Wendy wasn't too keen on having paths in the early years, when the garden was more of a secret,' remembers Corrado. 'She didn't want people coming in to stop her. So we all used to hop like goats from terrace to terrace. When the garden grew bigger and less secret, we put in the first entrance path and steps leading down, the one below the Moreton Bay fig. Then more paths and steps were added. But always narrow paths and steps on the scale of a domestic garden, never wide paths like the council park up top.'

'It was like winning a battle, when we finally stabilised and terraced that steep side of the valley.'

(*W W*)

The Gardeners

'The railway staff working in the yard beside the line always gave us a friendly wave. In the early years, when they were replacing railway sleepers on the line, they asked if we'd like the old ones.'

(RUBEN)

They listen with amusement as I relate that I'd read the original basis for determining the width of paths in Sydney's Royal Botanic Gardens. Paths were made wide enough to allow two ladies wearing hooped skirts to promenade side by side, pushing prams, and for others to approach and pass from the opposite direction.

'Oh glory, thank goodness we've moved on from hooped skirts and body-strangling corsets,' Wendy laughs.

Despite their worries that any day an official might arrive and tell them to stop trespassing, this never happened. 'On the contrary,' Ruben recalls. 'The railway staff working in the yard beside the line always gave us a friendly wave. In the early years, when they were replacing railway sleepers on the line, they asked if we'd like the old ones. We said, "Yes please," and they replied, "They're all yours".

'So we'd lug those heavy sleepers up the hillside to make terraces. Everything had to be carried by hand; we could never get trucks, cranes or bobcats in here. When we put the first picnic table and chairs in a nice spot in the garden, the railway workers asked if they could come and eat their lunch there, as it was so beautiful. We replied, "Help yourself, it's all yours!" Even the railway workers didn't realise this was railway land.'

While Wendy, Corrado and Ruben had started off as amateur gardeners, their confidence grew as they became more familiar with the site, learning the best way to rectify formidable problems, or take advantage of small triumphs. They became familiar with the serendipity of unlikely plants that would thrive in one spot, while others stubbornly refused to grow, or sulked and never flowered.

Wendy began to hire more part-time gardeners as the size and scope of the Secret Garden grew more ambitious. Several have stayed two or three years, then moved on in their travels or careers. In the early years, there was Chantal, an enthusiastic gardener from Holland; then Justin, who also worked in a native plant nursery and helped procure large quantities of native plants to start filling the bare terraces.

Luke Dewing, English and an avid surfer, began working in the garden and excelled in building dry stone walls, using the sandstone rubble. Luke won the heart of Keny's daughter, Francisca. They wed and have two children, and Luke now runs his own landscape business. Luke's friend, Nick Sandy, worked in the garden for some months. Nick took photographs and also collected photographs various people had taken of the early stages of clearing and making the Secret Garden, and made them into a self-published book. Several of those photographs appear on these pages.

TOP (*WW*) 'We cut up old railway sleepers to make the stairs as well, securing each step with lengths of angle iron. We place low-grade mulch on the steps and pathways, so you're not walking on mud. When this mulch eventually breaks down, it's 'cooked' in composting terms, and ready to be raked off and used as mulch on the garden beds.'

BOTTOM (*WW*) 'Luke excelled at building dry stone walls. There were tonnes of sandstone rubble at the far end of the garden, probably from smashing up the original sandstone cliffs to create landfill for the railway, so we rescued this and turned it back into something beautiful.'

The Gardeners

Corrado and Ruben busily at work, amidst banana palms, daturas, agaves and iresine.

(*CORRADO*) 'I like all these plants. The worst plants to prune or work closely with are the tree ferns. They look so beautiful, but drop fine brown powder which gives me an itchy rash.'

(**WW**) 'Visitors are very fond of our bush branch handrails. We put a lot of effort into making them aesthetically pleasing, to look at and to touch. We wrap zinc around the joints to conceal the screws. I love the effect. The wood often needs replacing, but it is increasingly difficult to acquire here. I'm getting a load from my friend Gary's place in Tasmania. *Can't wait*, and I am very grateful.'

'Rather like the composition in many of Brett's paintings, I prefer large areas of tranquillity with an intensity of interesting things happening around the edges.'

(*WW*)

Klara, who'd studied landscape design in her homeland, the Czech Republic, now works part-time in the Secret Garden and continues studying landscape design in Sydney. Jay Jay, Corrado's nephew, worked part-time in the garden and is studying horticulture. Jack, also a horticulture student, was another part-time member of the gardening team.

Ruben says, 'Wendy always worked a full day beside us. She'd dig and weed and carry broken glass. She'd keep going in the rain like we did, in gumboots and wet weather gear and get covered in mud and clay. She never played the princess.'

But, crucially, Wendy is also the garden artist, leading her team and continually fine-tuning her creation.

The Secret Garden spreads below the house, like a giant canvas she continues to paint daily. Instead of brushes and a palette of paints, she daubs with plants and trees, rocks and mulch.

'Rather like the composition in many of Brett's paintings,' Wendy explains. 'I prefer large areas of tranquillity with an intensity of interesting things happening around the edges. I don't want a jungle, with plants shoved in everywhere. It's a different kind of energy to leave calm spaces, where you can sit in the middle with a shaft of sunlight and contemplate all sorts of intricate things as you look around.

'It's also important to retain the strong sense of place here. So, at the top of the Secret Garden, you see Sydney Harbour. Coming down the entry steps, we keep the height of plants descending as you descend, so as not to block the harbour views. When you reach the bottom of the steps, you don't see the harbour at all, so the garden takes on a different atmosphere.'

Unlike a painting, a garden is never finished. A myriad of activities is involved in creating, enriching and tending a garden, and Wendy's mind is always ticking over.

She keeps seeing things to improve, shapes to enhance or simplify; new juxtapositions with different pairings of plants; new colour compositions. Wendy can become impassioned with a certain tree, like the *Magnolia grandiflora* with its fragrant, creamy-white, dish-sized flowers, and want more of them. Her vision is also ruthless. If things grow in ways that displease her eye, she moves or eliminates them.

It would be so much easier in a painting, just to take the turps rag and wipe out the unwanted section, then paint in a new version. No years of waiting for plants to grow as desired. 'I suppose this garden is more like making a sculpture than a painting, as it's three-dimensional,' Wendy observes.

Walking along with Wendy, I get a lecture in colour appreciation. 'I'm not fond of purple,' she comments. 'I use masses of iresine in the garden, but it's not purple, it's plum. Plum is not purple. I'm talking about blue purple, which is a bit harsh. I'm not fond of royal purple or bright purple either, it's got too much red and blue mixed together. That's the colour spectrum. Purple is nice in pansies, but that's got a lot to do with the light. I like lavender; it's mauve, not purple.'

The Gardeners

TOP Luke learnt a lot working in the Secret Garden, and has gone on to run his own successful landscaping business.

MIDDLE (*WW*) 'Chantal was a back-packer from Holland, and a great worker – very strong and very bright. We'd both often fall down the steep slopes, and she'd just laugh and pick herself up, and get on with it – as would I.'

BOTTOM (*WW*) 'Lunch break for Corrado and me with Helen Simons in the very early days, under the bamboo – one of the few places where there was any shade. Corrado has carried on the barbecue tradition, doing barbecues for the volunteers or, when they're lucky, pizzas.'

The Gardeners

(**WW**) 'Loved gardens flourish, and give pleasure and love back to those who love to spend time in them.

'I am totally against passive entertainment for kids; they need to be outdoors in nature to fully develop all their senses. Here in the garden children can just be; they can invent stories, be creative, and use their imaginations.'

'I use masses of iresine in the garden, but it's not purple, it's plum. Plum is not purple. I'm talking about blue purple, which is a bit harsh. I'm not fond of royal purple or bright purple either, it's got too much red and blue mixed together. That's the colour spectrum. Purple is nice in pansies, but that's got a lot to do with the light. I like lavender; it's mauve, not purple.'

(**WW**)

Wendy has a flair for taking a common, indeed scorned, plant that is easy to mass-propagate, and transforming it into a highly desirable one, by the way she 'paints' with it.

The prime example is *Iresine herbstii*, old-fashioned bloodleaf, which is almost the Secret Garden's signature plant, linking the whole colour field together. Boring old iresine, spurned and unloved, is also tagged 'the beefsteak plant', 'the cooked beetroot plant', and worse, 'the chicken gizzard plant'.

The iresine population explosion started with a single pot plant of it that Corrado had at his home in what he self-mockingly chuckles is, 'my wog garden; all pavers and pots'. Wendy wanted a low-growing plant with plum-coloured leaves, to cut a swathe through the various greens and silvery-leafed plants. So Corrado snapped several stalks off his single pot plant and propagated them. Iresine is so easy to propagate and grows so rapidly, even a black-thumbed non-gardener could grow it.

'I didn't much like iresine at first,' Wendy admits. 'Its waxy leaves reminded me of those wax plants our grandmothers used to grow; but now I cherish it. I love clumping iresine against light green, strappy-leafed bird's nest ferns and feathery silver-grey foliage. When the sun strikes the plum-coloured leaves, a luminous sheen glows like amethyst. Look more closely at the leaves; the intensity of the reds differs, from crimson to dark wine, and you'll see an interesting pattern of pink veins.'

Multiple swathes of iresine now weave a richly coloured harmony throughout the Secret Garden, and sunlight streaming through the deep red foliage is like sun beaming through stained glass windows. All this from Corrado's one unloved pot plant. Over a picnic lunch, we discuss what a miraculous thing it is, to propagate plants from cuttings; plus it brings enormous pleasure to get thousands of plants for free.

Wendy became besotted with the sight of massed white hydrangeas at Lake Maggiore during a trip to Italy, so clumps of white hydrangeas are now dancing through the Secret Garden like *Swan Lake* chorus lines. Corrado valiantly tried to propagate one hundred white hydrangea cuttings, but a strange mould infected them and most stubbornly refused to strike.

He might not have had much luck with his hydrangea cuttings, but he enjoys success with his vegie patches in various sunny nooks in the Secret Garden. Salad greens, peas, beans, tomatoes, spinach, zucchini, cucumbers and herbs all flourish. Likewise strawberry patches and many citrus trees. He loves trees and plants that produce food. 'Look at this grapefruit tree. He's so heavy with fruit, his branches are almost breaking,' Corrado will say admiringly. To Corrado, all plants are 'he'.

Visitors to the garden are welcome to pick a small quantity of fruit and vegetables to enjoy, and the gardeners encourage children to see the food growing.

'Kids today think lettuce grows in plastic bags, just like you see it on the supermarket shelf,' Ruben laments.

(**WW**) 'Iresine has been amazingly helpful in the palette I've used to "paint" the Secret Garden, indeed it's hard to know what I might have done without it.

'Iresine is not the sort of plant I really would have used, but I wanted a plum-red colour and Corrado gave me some cuttings from a single pot plant of iresine he had at home in what he mirthfully calls his "wog garden" of pot plants, and they just took off.

'I like the way it has introduced colour into what is predominantly a green garden. You do have to prune it regularly though, otherwise it can go mad and take over. We use the prunings to propagate more iresine.'

OPPOSITE (*WW*) 'Corrado loves citrus – he has planted lemons, oranges, pink grapefruit, blood oranges, cumquats and limes.

'I have made cumquat jam, and one of the volunteers makes grapefruit jam. Corrado loves trees that are productive – that bear fruit rather than flowers. He's also planted guava, quince, pomegranate and mulberries.'

LEFT One of Corrado's small vegie gardens – he loves growing zucchini, tomatoes, rocket, asparagus, cucumbers and chilli in sunny spots.

When the odd visitor gets too keen on picking, and produces a bag to fill with all the mandarins from a tree, or takes all the strawberries in a patch, Corrado will voice a firm reminder that it's there for everyone to share, so just take a little please.

Corrado also likes a joke. A friend arrived early to meet me in the garden, and came across Corrado raking a large, bare patch of new topsoil underneath the Moreton Bay fig tree. My friend Joy paused to admire his meticulous raking, and inquired, 'What are you going to do here?'

Corrado: 'I'm making a new vegie garden. I'm going to plant tomatoes, rocket, spinach, and watch my vegies grow.'

Joy, politely: 'But there isn't enough sun here. I grow vegetables, and they need full sun.'

Corrado, smile glinting: 'Yes, that's right, vegies need a lotta sun. So you see this house behind me, the lady's tall house with the balcony and tower? It's blocking the sun, so I'm going to knock it down so I can have sun on my vegie patch all day.'

Joy burst into laughter, and Corrado walked off, laughing like a rogue, and whistling happily as he began to unload a trailer full of new turf to lay beneath the Moreton Bay fig on the prepared soil.

Corrado's one frustration with his fruit and vegetable produce in the Secret Garden is that he cannot use insect sprays. Periodically, fruit flies invade the fruit trees, and white cabbage moths do their maddening catch-me-if-you-can dance, laying eggs and shrivelling the leaves on his salad greens. 'I cannot spray, because you can't eat anything for several days after you spray, and no matter if we put one of Ruben's friendly signs up saying, "Please don't eat this because it's just been sprayed," someone might ignore the sign.'

As alluded to earlier, like any family, the gardeners and Wendy all have their 'moments'. Both heated and cool 'moments' generally arise out of Wendy's desire for change. Corrado says, 'Wendy likes to change things: the garden, the inside of the house, her clothes, and her cars. She's the boss, the artist, the architect, the curator, the head gardener – she does everything – and she always wants change. It never stays the same. After a few years I do start to wonder: why does Wendy always change her mind? Why does she always want us to move plants, move paths, move steps, move trees?

'Maybe the tree has grown and Wendy doesn't like the way it looks in that position now. She'll say the shape or colour doesn't match, it doesn't get enough sun, or it needs more shade, or she doesn't like the look of it now. It's always "the look" and "Use your eyes."'

'Even if the plant is 100 per cent right; it's growing well and the colours are right – Wendy wants to take it out today and try something new! She decides the look of that earlier set of steps is wrong – she wants more distance between each step, or the staircase curved 5 per cent more to the right, so it will look better. She wants the terraces to curve more, like a snake, no straight lines. After so many years, we know very well what Wendy likes, and dislikes. Nothing can be in a straight line – it's always curves, waves, undulating shapes.'

'Look at this grapefruit tree. He's so heavy with fruit, his branches are almost breaking.'

(*CORRADO*)

The Gardeners

Ruben enjoying the serenity, as he meticulously selects stones he brought from Hill End to build a small monument as a tribute to all the artists who work there.

'After so many years, we know very well what Wendy likes, and dislikes. Nothing can be in a straight line – it's always curves, waves, undulating shapes.'

(CORRADO)

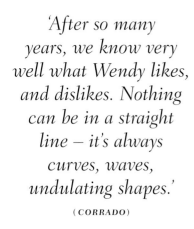

Wendy remarks that she dislikes gardens resembling neat parade grounds organised by drill sergeants. 'No rows of marching soldiers allowed here, thank you!' She readily admits to being 'an obsessive perfectionist, highly self-critical, impatient and bossy' about how she wants things done in the garden.

Corrado concurs. 'Sometimes it drives us crazy. But you cannot change the person; that's the way she is. Wendy is very creative, and I'm very, very happy with the result. I think the Secret Garden is beautiful.'

That said, tempers have been known to fray. 'We have had a few blow-ups, sure,' Corrado admits. 'I used to argue that things could not be done. I'd say, "Wendy, we cannot lift that huge rock from here to there, it's too hard, and it won't look good anyway." Or I'd say, "That tree is too big to dig out and move, it won't survive being transplanted, it will die."

'Wendy will insist it *can* be done. I'm thinking this is *impossible*, and Wendy is insisting it *is possible.* So we might have a blow-up. If I need to say something, I say it; and Wendy is the same. Then we all cool down, and it's OK.'

Ruben likewise praises Wendy's skills, saying, 'She has such a good eye, I've learned so much from her about composition, what goes with what, placement, and revealing special qualities. For instance, Wendy will sometimes have us clear around a certain tree so you can appreciate the form of the trunk and the patterns in the bark. When we unearth a large loose boulder, Wendy has taught us instead of leaving it flat, to turn the rock upright on its side, so it becomes a piece of sculpture. We might shift it slightly twenty times till she's satisfied it looks right.'

But occasionally he becomes frustrated when he feels Wendy's determination goes to extremes. Rolling his eyes heavenwards, Ruben exclaims, 'I mean, placing plants is not like placing pieces of furniture! Plants keep growing bigger. Sometimes we plant a young tree exactly where Wendy tells us, knowing it looks right now, but in a few years it will have to be moved, because it's too close to the next trees and it's going to take over.

'So, in three years' time, Wendy will come along and look critically at this taller tree and ask, "Who planted this here?"

'We'll plead, "But Wendy, you told us to plant it here". She'll reply, "Well, I don't like it here now, it needs moving."' Ruben grins and shakes his head, 'So we move it.'

Only once has Ruben become totally exasperated, when Wendy decided to move two advanced tree ferns a few metres to the right.

'Four tree ferns had grown tall, with thick trunks and wonderful arching fronds, under the big coral tree,' he begins. 'Then, one day, Wendy decides she wants to move two of these big tree ferns over to the right, where she has none. It would look better.

'We try to say, "Wendy, these tree ferns are too big and too heavy. They've grown enormous root balls embedded in amongst huge rocks and other tree root systems. It's a massive job to even try to dig them out. We'd need a bulldozer and a crane to move them, but you know we can't get machinery in here."

The Gardeners

Corrado (**LEFT**) carefully honing one of the bush-branch handrails and Ruben (**RIGHT**) hand-painting a friendly sign asking visitors to please take their rubbish with them. Wendy's gardeners have more than enough to do without having to collect the public's rubbish.

'But Wendy says, "Well, we'll just do a massive job by ourselves then, won't we!"

'So four of us – Corrado, Luke, me and Wendy – are all digging with crowbars and spades and picks, trying to wedge the huge root balls out, so we can move these two tree ferns. It took almost three days' work to do it. The same guy used to come every day and sit nearby, reading a book and eating his lunch, watching us struggling with spades and ropes. He's probably thinking, "Why on earth are they doing this?" and in the back of our minds we're thinking the same thing. Surely it's not worth all this effort. Why doesn't Wendy just buy two new tree ferns and plant them over there? But Wendy had a vision of what she wanted to achieve, and having started this exercise she wasn't going to quit. You have to admire her for that!'

The unfortunate postscript is that one of the transplanted tree ferns died, and the other one looked sick for the next four years, then it died too. 'You get a marvellous pattern, like a giraffe, when tree ferns die and the furry growth falls off the trunk, so I've left a few like that,' Wendy notes, defensively.

'When things like this happen, it's best to say nothing, and just get on with it,' Ruben adds wisely. 'The thing about Wendy is that she is unique. She is obsessive to the maximum; I've never known any person like her. But her obsession has its origins in her ability to understand form and beauty. Everything around her must have perfect form and beauty, she won't settle for second rate. So you forgive her almost everything, because it's what makes up her whole personality.

'And I love the Secret Garden. I truly love it. Corrado and I watch all the trees and plants growing like they're our children, and when one gets sickly or dies, we are very sad.'

It's Ruben who paints the friendly, handmade signs placed discreetly through the garden, 'Please take your rubbish away with you', or 'Please clean up after yourself and your dog'. (Wendy and her gardeners must do all the public rubbish collection inside the Secret Garden.)

Ruben says, 'When I go back on holidays to Uruguay to see my family, I miss Wendy's garden. I'm always checking on the internet to see if some visitor has put up new photographs. I'm always thinking about it. A picture of that garden is permanently painted inside my mind.'

Still, the gardeners aren't beyond hatching a mini-rebellion. Ruben discloses one triumph.

'Everything in the Secret Garden has to be carried in by hand, in a bag or a wheelbarrow,' he begins. 'So we have to carry trees, soil, fertilisers, sprays – everything we need, from the top down to the bottom. Then we have to carry all the weeds and dead leaves, pruning offcuts, and other rubbish, back up to the top. We tie the heavy load onto the wheelbarrow, so it won't fall off. For many years we only had steps going from the bottom to the top.

'It was a nightmare, walking backwards up the steep slope with the wheelbarrow, one step at a time, me carrying the handles and Corrado lifting the wheel, to go bump, bump up the steps, all the way to the top. We'd been trying to persuade Wendy to let us build a zigzag track up the hillside, with no steps, so we could wheel the barrows up and down. So much easier than steps. But Wendy didn't like the idea of this visually; she said there were already too many paths and that the shape wouldn't look right. Maybe she'd see about it later on.'

'Her obsession has its origins in her ability to understand form and beauty. Everything around her must have perfect form and beauty, she won't settle for second rate.'

(*RUBEN*)

The Gardeners

The times when tempers fray and wills clash are when Wendy, as Corrado and Ruben put it, 'decides to move trees around like pieces of furniture!'

One example: A large coral tree had been cut down, and its stump left rotting in the ground. Wendy decided it was time the stump was dug out, and a mature datura moved into its place.

Corrado, Jack and Jay Jay dug out the stump while Wendy selected a datura to dig up and transplant into the hole.

(**CORRADO**) 'Not so simple, eh? Wendy is standing back, looking at this transplanted datura from every angle, and calling out to us to move it round, this way, more, no back a bit. Then we wait while she walks to yet another angle, and yells out for us to twist it round again.

'Finally she's happy. We reckoned it looked good the first way we put it in the hole – but She's the Boss, Wendy is always the Boss.'

At last, Wendy's transplant surgery completed, Corrado wheels away the offending stump.

'Wendy likes to change things: the garden, the inside of the house, her clothes, and her cars. She's the Boss, the artist, the architect, the curator, the head gardener – she does everything – and she always wants change.'

(CORRADO)

The Gardeners

The now applauded zigzag path.
The gardeners hatched a mini-rebellion when Wendy was away on holidays, building the step-free zigzag path they had long wanted but Wendy had opposed, arguing it might be pragmatic but it wouldn't work aesthetically.
But it did work on both counts, Wendy agreed when she saw it. (**WW**) 'So, one up for the gardeners!'

OPPOSITE (*WW*) 'Mr Handsome.
'When I slid down the cliff into the
brambles, I decided to hire my first
strong helper, Corrado. He's still
working with me, and loves the
Secret Garden as much as I do.'

(*CORRADO*) 'Wendy's garden is
a collaboration with her gardening
team – only She's the Boss. After over
twenty years, Ruben and I still can't
pick what she's going to change today,
what new idea she wants to try.
Believe me, there's no one like Wendy.'

LEFT One of the young bottle trees
on the zigzag path, its trunk swollen
with stored water.

In 2008, Wendy went to England for three months. Ruben's face gleams, remembering,
'Corrado and I decide, right, we're gonna make that zigzag path while she's away. We'll make it
look so good that she'll leave it there.' And that's what happened. Plus, visitors pushing babies
in prams and strollers loved the zigzag path and started using it too.

Though one day I was in the garden with Wendy, near the bottom of the zigzag path, and she
paused, and stared up at it, frowning. 'I don't like that section up on the left there,' she pointed
out. 'You see those two long, bare railway sleepers stacked on top of each other – it's visually
wrong from this angle. I'll get the gardeners to pull out the bottom sleeper and replace it with
stones, which will be far more pleasing to the eye.'

I thought of asking, 'Wouldn't it be easier to grow a creeper over the offending railway
sleeper?' but figured I'd get a disapproving 'Hmmmph'.

Later I walked up the reconfigured zigzag path with Corrado, then along a side path, which
leads beside three bottle trees. The bottle trees look marvellous growing right beside the track,
their cool, swollen trunks full of stored water.

'But Corrado,' I venture, 'I've seen bottle trees with trunks over 2 metres wide out in the
bush. What are you going to do if these start growing bigger and totally block the path? They'll
be too huge to move.'

Corrado throws back his head and laughs richly.

'Don't worry, Wendy will try.'

*'Corrado and
I decide, right, we're
gonna make that
zigzag path while she's
away. We'll make it
look so good that she'll
leave it there.'*

(*RUBEN*)

(*WW*) 'True optical ecstasy. Elating. A natural high; the best high of all.'

EASIER

Through the Eyes of Friends

Gary Topping, fellow passionate
gardener, who inspired the
Mediterranean garden of lavender,
rosemary, sage and thyme at the top
border, where the Secret Garden
meets Clark Park.

Wendy is rarely at home alone. As well as her team of gardeners six days a week, and loyal housekeeper Keny, a group of close old friends who live overseas or interstate are regular houseguests.

Wendy's friends are all in creative fields: art, music, film, theatre, dance, design – writers, poets, photographers and publishers, along with amateur and professional gardeners. Several old friends call Wendy 'Weet' or 'Weetie', the pet name Brett gave her. All have keenly watched the evolution of the Secret Garden.

GARY TOPPING

The regular guest with the most intimate connection to the garden is Gary Topping. He has helped periodically from the start. Gary planted the earliest defining border – the Mediterranean garden – the long strip across the top of the valley where the Secret Garden meets the more formal lawns of Clark Park.

The name evolved because conditions there are hotter and drier, so he planted Mediterranean-style lavenders, rosemary, salvias and echium, which flower in a wash of blues and mauves.

Gary is a tall, strongly built man, with a kind heart, generous nature and a warm apple-cheeked smile. These days he and his partner, architect Zak Syvaniemi, enjoy a pleasant lifestyle, dividing their time between garden-lapped homes in Tuscany and Tasmania, with regular stays at Wendy's, where Gary will happily toil away in the garden.

Gary has always felt a strong empathy with Wendy's Secret Garden journey, as it parallels events that unfolded in his own personal life. He's not alone in this: the story of Wendy's Secret Garden seems to deeply touch many people in their own private way.

In Gary's case, like Wendy, he was caught in a tsunami of grief in 1992 following the loss of his then partner, and threw himself into making a large garden. As with Wendy, it started him on a path to becoming a self-taught, ongoing, passionate gardener.

It's a crisp autumn morning, the sun is glimmering on Lavender Bay, and Wendy, Gary and Zak are finishing their breakfast muesli and coffee in the kitchen as I arrive.

I'd been to the late Margaret Olley's Paddington house the previous day, to collect cuttings and plants from her overgrown garden. The beloved still life painter and arts benefactor, known in the art world as 'Queen Oll', had died and her house was going to auction. Wendy had purchased the Italianate Cupid fountain which sat in Olley's garden amidst a pond of Japanese irises and lilies, so I'd gathered some of these irises and lilies to plant beside the fountain in its new home in Wendy's garden.

Through the Eyes of Friends

(**WW**) 'Gary and Corrado both love pruning – they vie to get their hands on the chainsaw. I was always very tentative about pruning, but Gary was the gardeners' ally in this argument, insisting I see that pruning really works. He severely pruned some old mulberry trees back into beautiful shapes to convince me.'

(**GARY**) 'There are so many memories in Wendy's Secret Garden – hers, Brett's, Arkie's and all the people who've helped make the garden. And what was here, before the garden. It makes you think about the fragile and ephemeral nature of memory.'

'Corrado had started working for Wendy, and I remember saying to him, "Wow, let's keep going and make the garden bigger."'

(**GARY**)

Wendy is eager to get down to the garden to start placing the Olley plants. Gary makes more coffee and we linger, talking. Like all Wendy's friends, Gary has led an interesting life with a lot of movement.

Sydney-born in 1948, after graduating in economics he left to work in New York when he was in his twenties, then moved to the Alabama Gulf Coast, where he ran a highly successful specialist travel agency for clients in advertising, fashion and publishing. Gary and his then long-time partner, an American writer, lived in a fine old home on 9 hectares, with a garden of huge old magnolia trees.

'We had a wonderful life,' Gary says, 'but my partner suddenly became ill and died in 1992 (the same year that Brett died).

'I was devastated, really lost. I didn't know what to do and lived in a void.' His voice shakes; the memories cut deep. 'A friend had bought a holiday house in Tuscany,' Gary continues, 'and she said, "Why don't you go to the house and have some time off? Build a garden or something. The house doesn't have a garden and could do with one."

'So I took five months off work, went to live in Tuscany, became a hermit, and built the garden from scratch. It was very healing. I was exhausted at the end of each day, but I was throwing myself into something totally different. It was a rough site and I was building walkways and steps, working out perspectives and planting. I enjoyed the solitude and close contact with nature; sometimes it was elating. I was on the edge of turning into a full-time hermit.

'I remember one day being on the top terrace, staring at the sky and watching the clouds go by, and thinking to myself: I've gotta stop this, and get back to some sort of reality.

'I was so enjoying the creativity, the physical work, the calmness of working in the dirt. I'd become obsessive about the garden. From the moment I woke up, I couldn't wait to finish what I'd started yesterday, and to get a new task underway.'

He went back to America, then returned to Tuscany the following year for another five months to complete the garden. The next year he came to Sydney on a holiday and visited Wendy.

'She'd just started the Secret Garden, and I offered to help. I said, "Let me have the top part where it's hot and dry and the soil is sandy, and I can plant a Mediterranean garden like I have in Tuscany. We could have a sweet-smelling garden of lavender, rosemary, sage and thyme."

'But the soil here was terrible, basically broken-down sandstone rocks with no organic matter. I'd be digging a hole in the rubble, picking out broken bottles, old taps, paint tins, pipes, then adding pockets of new soil and mulch for planting. Gradually, I got the top garden growing, then added day lilies, proteas, euphorbias and birds of paradise.' In this poorer soil, Gary coaxed echium to flourish, and tall cobalt blue spires of echium flower spectacularly for months, above the lavenders.

Gary continues, 'Corrado had started working for Wendy, and I remember saying to him, "Wow, let's keep going and make the garden bigger". I remember clearing under the big Port

Through the Eyes of Friends

'I could see that the garden was healing Wendy, but we didn't discuss it much at first.'

(GARY)

Jackson fig tree, which had this mass of tall lantana and vines strangling it and smothering the ground. We kept clearing down to this fabulous flat rock shelf where you could now stand and look out to Sydney Harbour. There was an almost spiritual feeling to it, as you wondered who'd stood here in earlier centuries. Each day was like a voyage of discovery.

'I could see that the garden was healing Wendy, but we didn't discuss it much at first. We were both obsessive about staying outside working. We'd wander out in the morning at first light, prowling around, still in our pyjamas, and start weeding and get covered in dirt. Then we'd be outside working till after dark, struck by the nocturnal magic of it all, and need torch-light to come inside.'

Gary continued his regular gardening visits, staying with Wendy for a month over Christmas and a couple of times during the year.

'When Arkie died in 2001, I was heartbroken for Weet. I just wanted to pick her up and hold her,' he says. 'We talked about grieving after Arkie died. When you lose someone so precious, you feel so spun-out and lost. People say, "Oh it gets better with time". That's bullshit. It never gets better. You get used to it. It's always part of you. You never forget them. They come across your mind and memory every day in some way. Wendy and I were both hiding from the world in our gardens, burying our hearts and souls in the gardens and seeking solace.'

Gary mentions something else that gave Wendy simple solace – Arkie's two small dogs. At that point Wendy had four small dogs, two of her own and two of Arkie's. It was an ongoing affectionate connection, something of Arkie's still living to hug and watch as they happily wagged tails and romped around.

'Wendy is a strong woman, she never feels sorry for herself, she keeps her feelings locked deep inside her,' says Gary. 'To see things growing gives you hope. I walk around the garden now and recall when it was a wasteland and we'd wonder how in hell's name you'd ever get

Through the Eyes of Friends

(*GARY*) 'We'd wander out in the morning at first light, prowling around, still in our pyjamas, and start weeding and get covered in dirt. Then we'd be outside working till after dark, struck by the nocturnal magic of it all, and need torchlight to come inside.'

'Look, those trees
must be pruned or
cut down. I'll take the
heat; let's get to work
while Wendy is
busy elsewhere.'

(*GARY*)

anything growing here. I remember planting these trees when they were so tiny, and now they've grown so tall. Umpteen times I slid down the hillside, through broken glass, sharp, rusty metal and foul rubbish. I remember Weet and myself planting all the jacarandas to commemorate Arkie, then huge rains came, and half the hillside, including all the new jacarandas, slid towards the bottom of the valley. So we propped them up, secured them with rock walls and replanted them where they landed. They've all survived and thrived.'

Indeed, the garden thrived so well in its own new microclimate that the problem Wendy herself now acknowledges is that she too zealously overplanted. Considerable judicious pruning and thinning is now required, as taller trees are smothering the understorey and blocking too much sunlight.

Gary explains with an affectionate laugh, 'Weet used to go crazy in the early years if I wanted to prune the lower branches off a tree to give it a better growing shape, or prune higher branches to let the sun come in. She was this Earth Mother figure who'd reared her precious trees, and wouldn't let you touch a limb of one of her children. I totally understand – I can't pick a flower in my own garden, as it will spoil the pleasure of seeing it continue to grow.'

Gary became the gardeners' pruning ally. Corrado and Ruben would be longing to prune particular trees, but fear Wendy's wrath, so would await Gary's next visit.

Gary, 'I'd say to Ruben and Corrado, "Look, those trees must be pruned or cut down. I'll take the heat; let's get to work while Wendy is busy elsewhere."'

Fortunately Wendy usually approved of Gary's aesthetic pruning, began to agree it was needed, and has herself now become an enthusiastic pruner, especially to create sight lines and windows through the mature garden.

Gary's technique of pruning lavender is much admired. He can make a lavender look magnificent for twelve to fifteen years before it goes straggly. He gives lavender a severe prune at the end of summer, when the flowers have died down and the bees departed. Then he lifts up the heavy bottom branches like a dowager's skirt and trims these off to expose the trunk, so the bush grows like a small squat tree.

Gary is also the gardeners' ally on the touchy subject of Wendy wanting to 'move trees around like pieces of furniture' as the garden grows.

He chortles, 'Oh, it's often quite a game. I remember grand feuds over moving a mulberry tree and an olive tree to new spots. Me backing the gardeners, arguing, "The mulberry tree

Through the Eyes of Friends

will get too big there, and the olive tree won't grow well there". And Weet saying, "Well I want them moved, I will like them better over there; they don't look right any more where they are now".

'And round in circles we'd go, me backing the gardeners and Weet decrying, "No! No!"'

'Someone gave Wendy several cocos palms that were bursting their pots on a balcony, and she wanted to plant them near the big tipping cliff. I said to Weet, "They will get huge and be a nuisance," and she insisted, "No they won't, and besides I like them."'

Fifteen years on, the cocos palms were so huge, collapsing and taking up so much room, that they were felled and removed on one of Gary's visits. Wendy finally concurred that the cocos palms had served their role and it was time for them to go.

'Gardening is good for the head, as well as for the body and soul,' Gary maintains, with a cheery smile. 'You can have a million things going on in your life, then you get in your garden and forget them and go into a meditative zone.

'You start to think calmly about something else. Your eyes notice things with a new clarity ... like the glorious shapes in a flower's face, or a bug you haven't seen before. Suddenly you are looking at this amazing coloured bug on a leaf, and the bug is looking at you, and you're thinking, "Hello new bug, what sort of a bug are you?"'

'When I'm back in Tuscany and Tasmania, I'm still always thinking of Wendy's garden and how it's going, and can't wait to get back into it.

'I often imagine Lavender Bay in its historical context, because I feel the historical echoes when I'm in the Secret Garden looking across to Sydney Harbour. I think how it must have been when the Aborigines watched the First Fleet sail in, and what life was like for the convicts transported from England. I think about the original harbour inlet beach that was here, and now lies buried deep beneath the Secret Garden, after all that landfill was dumped over the beach to build the railway. Lavender Bay is a vast repository of memories.

'In my younger years I often sailed on Sydney Harbour, and we'd bring the yacht over to Lavender Bay to get the engine serviced. There were boatsheds with boats being winched up into cradles, and skilled boat-building activity all around the bay. That's all gone now.'

Like Wendy, Gary had a treasured childhood secret garden.

'My grandmother had a lovely old garden in Mosman, and I had my secret garden there, a piece of the garden I regarded as *mine*.

'It was behind a huge camphor laurel tree; you went two steps down to sit on the giant roots of the tree, near some old-fashioned roses. It was my hideout, I could go there to be by myself. I didn't have a dog, so I talked to my imaginary friends and my teddy bear. My parents were going through a horrible divorce, and it was a very important place for me to go and seek solace. The hair on my teddy bear was almost worn off, I cuddled it so much. The memory of that small haven has stayed with me. Perhaps that's why so many of us seek a secret garden again, later in our adult lives.'

'Your eyes notice things with a new clarity ... like the glorious shapes in a flower's face, or a bug you haven't seen before. Suddenly you are looking at this amazing coloured bug on a leaf, and the bug is looking at you, and you're thinking, "Hello new bug, what sort of a bug are you?"'

(GARY)

ANNA SCHWARTZ

Anna Schwartz, the forever glamorous proprietor of Anna Schwartz Gallery in Sydney and Melbourne, is one of Wendy's oldest, closest friends.

Like Wendy, Anna is a walking work of art herself, her slender body always garbed in strikingly original clothes and contemporary jewellery. Also like Wendy, Anna has a sharply intelligent mind, a strong aesthetic sense, and a warm and wise personality.

Anna has known Brett and Wendy since 1970, when she was nineteen; the same year she met her first husband, sculptor Joel Elenberg, who tragically died from lymphoma ten years later, aged only thirty-two. Brett and Joel were best friends, and an intense bond soon formed between all four, strengthened by their shared passion for art.

Before Joel died, Whiteley painted his friend's suffering in a crucifixion series. After Joel died, Whiteley painted *The Letter (To Anna) 1980–81*, depicting Anna lying naked on a couch, with a letter and a small bunch of violets on the floor beside her. Anna says, 'I didn't pose for the portrait, and it wasn't an actual letter. It was symbolic; life's letter to you. It's a deeply felt painting.'

Anna arrives every month to stay with Wendy, while she attends to her Sydney gallery. 'I've known Wendy and Brett since Arkie was three, and seen so much of their lives unfold,' this loyal friend says, with deep affection. 'The highs and lows, joys and tragedies; the explorations.'

She holds vivid memories of the early years when Brett, Wendy and Arkie lived at Lavender Bay.

'Brett and Weet always lived their lives with extraordinary intensity, it was a high-octane relationship,' Anna recounts. 'Brett did everything to extremes; his art was extremely powerful and beautiful. He articulated Australia's sensual, summery nature. He was magnetic, lovable and very forgivable, because of his seething talent and inquiring mind.

'He was an endlessly demanding storm of energy, so Weet had no chance to even contemplate making a garden while she was preoccupied with being the artist's wife, intrinsically involved in Brett's work.'

Gazing at the Secret Garden from Wendy's balcony, Anna remembers, 'It used to look so scary down here, unkempt and quite dangerous, you'd never have put a foot in there. It's extraordinary the way Wendy has taken a derelict site that had been crying out to be rescued, and injected beauty, depth of meaning and a sense of peace into it'.

While others see Wendy's garden as a giant painting, or a magnificent living oriental carpet, Anna sees it as 'a great piece of performance art'.

'Every sight line is fabulous,' she expands. 'Wendy so understands depth of field, placement, sequence. It's like a poem, with a sequence of rooms and spaces that reveal themselves, then close, and then the next space opens to reveal itself.

'When I walk into this garden, it appears to be the most wonderfully spontaneous organic setting, yet I know how it is all so carefully planned, with disciplined artistic thought.

'Every sight line is fabulous. Wendy so understands depth of field, placement, sequence. It's like a poem, with a sequence of rooms and spaces that reveal themselves, then close, and then the next space opens to reveal itself.'

(*ANNA*)

'At the same time, like the best artworks, it has a freedom of spirit that allows for any kind of accident or eventuality to have its place too.'

Anna loves the way Wendy had the courage and clarity of vision to do all this, 'without bothering about rules and regulations and complications. She's turned a hostile dump into a glorious experience for the public, and spent millions of dollars and thousands of hours of labour doing so. I can't think of anyone else who would have engaged in such an act, without a big fanfare of publicity for their philanthropy.

'Wendy has done it for very private reasons, with great integrity and humility. She's had so much loss in her life, and here she is surrounded by so much creation and new life. It has become her daily way of living; she comes down from the house to tend her garden and watches people come in to enjoy it, all in their own ways.'

We go down from the house to the Moreton Bay fig tree. It now carries so much history and memory, it seems like the Secret Garden's defining soul. Anna approaches Joel Elenberg's sculpture, and gently runs her supple fingers over the noble head.

While I'm talking to Anna as we sit under this old oracle tree, an array of different folk arrive and wander down into the Secret Garden. Two lovers with a picnic rug, a girl with a book and her lunch, three Vietnamese mothers in cheongsams with toddlers holding balloons. A father with his baby in a backpack-carrier. A group of students with swags of notes; it's a popular place to study, or just to contemplate. A small wedding is setting up, with a string quartet. An attendant is tying bunches of flowers to the trees with long, white ribbons, and has a bundle of white parasols to hand to guests.

It's a gorgeous, sunny, blue-sky day, and the garden below is almost looking astonished at its own lusty beauty.

Explosions of blooms seem to be on every plant, flirting with nectar-seeking birds. The daturas are crammed with chandeliers of apricot flowers; tresses of clotted-cream blossoms festoon the crepe myrtles. Necklaces of gleaming bronze seeds adorn the Bangalow palms. Freshly sprouted green leaves dance in the slight breeze.

Anna stretches both arms ahead at this garden composition, with the Brett Whiteley wooden sculpture *Nude* rising amidst it, and says, 'Just look at that vision – the impact is so voluptuous and sensual, with the plants nudging and undulating, giving the space an intimate calm, it's almost as if we're looking at a Brett Whiteley painting.

'It proves a point I have long made,' Anna continues. 'It is so obvious that Wendy's aesthetic eye was extremely important to Brett's work. Very often it was Wendy's way of configuring reality, her way of seeing things, her aesthetic sensibility that Brett was painting – infused with a lot of other things as well. But it was a very mutual vision.

'It has always been an instinctive trait in Weet, to make the world around her beautiful. She'll walk into a room, any space indoors or outdoors that she inhabits, and start curating and reconfiguring it, to endow it with aesthetic order.

'Just look at that vision – the impact is so voluptuous and sensual, with the plants nudging and undulating, giving the space an intimate calm, it's almost as if we're looking at a Brett Whiteley painting.'

(ANNA)

(*ANNA*) 'It's been Wendy's way of life for over twenty years now. She comes out of her house each day and works to make the Secret Garden an ever more appealing place for everyone to enjoy.'

Through the Eyes of Friends

'If Brett were here today he'd be painting the garden, using elements of it, transfiguring and reforming it. I think it would have been a huge addition to his oeuvre, a continuing of his celebrated Lavender Bay interiors and exteriors.'

(**ANNA**)

'Her home is a supreme exemplification of this. The choice and placement of objects, how she arranges a dish of food, how she puts things in context … a tribal mask, a rug, a chair, a painting … how she arranges a tableau.

'In Brett's Lavender Bay series, every colour and line in the house that he put into his paintings was made by Wendy. Every view was one that she had framed.

'It seemed like a natural progression for Wendy to continue beyond the house, to transform the horrible dump into a garden paradise, and create aesthetic life where there was none.

'If Brett were here today he'd be painting the garden, using elements of it, transfiguring and reforming it. I think it would have been a huge addition to his oeuvre, a continuing of his celebrated Lavender Bay interiors and exteriors.'

Anna too had her own childhood secret garden. 'I grew up in Beaumaris, a suburb on Port Phillip Bay in south-east Melbourne. It was then unmade roads and gumtrees, and at the back of our block was bushland,' she relates.

'I was very agile, so I used to climb over our high wooden paling back fence, then jump down into the bush and nobody knew I was there. I'd sit in the long grass and hide. It was wild and a bit scary, but it was the idea of being unfindable that was alluring. I think a lot of us have that primitive instinct to find your own private burrow where you go, just to be free. A self-discovery time.

'Wendy understands this, with her generous heart, and has deliberately made numerous spaces in the Secret Garden that can be small private zones.'

As we leave, Anna reflects, 'The more established the Secret Garden becomes, the more I see it as a public artwork, with Wendy as its artist and head gardener'.

Brett Whiteley scholar, Barry Pearce, Emeritus Curator of Australian Art at the Art Gallery of New South Wales, is a longtime friend and supporter of the Whiteleys.

(**BARRY**) 'Each time I visit the mysterious depths and surprises of this garden, I feel I am exploring deeper aspects of myself.'

BARRY PEARCE

Barry Pearce, now Emeritus Curator of Australian Art at the Art Gallery of New South Wales, has known Brett and Wendy Whiteley since the seventies.

Barry, a much-loved figure due to his passion for enhancing people's lives through art, holds vivid memories of their first encounter, when he was a shy young curator. 'Brett was bouncing on the balls of his feet, like a man on embers. Wendy was so imposingly beautiful, I could hardly broach a conversation.'

He has a sadder memory of Brett, coming to his office at the gallery in 1992 only a few weeks before the artist died. During that visit, Barry, as Curator of Australian Art, proposed that the gallery hold a major retrospective of Whiteley's work. A week later Barry visited Brett at his studio to discuss details.

After Brett's sudden death, Barry and Wendy were virtually thrown together to co-curate the retrospective, held in 1995.

'For all its travails, I am glad that exhibition happened,' says Barry, 'as, otherwise, I may never have gotten to know the extraordinary Wendy Whiteley. Difficult, obsessed, analytical to the point of pain, yet compassionate, humorous and highly intelligent. In those same years, out of a railway rubbish dump, she single-handedly began to create a garden that may well be the most precious private haven in Sydney.'

During 1994, Wendy and Barry met at the Lavender Bay house frequently to plan the retrospective. 'The house was filled with Brett's work and decorated with Wendy's distinctive Arabian Nights mystique. Then there was *that* view of Sydney Harbour, the liquid heart of the city, from the living room balcony. Astonishing, mesmerising,' Barry recalls.

'All the more so, when the trees were then less obstructive, so one didn't really notice the rubbish dump in the gorge below the house, because your gaze was so held above it and beyond. Moreover, the horrible debris from countless years of neglect was obscured by layers of weed and creepers.

'Wendy had taken notice though, as she started to tidy up the edges and place a few pieces of sculpture on the lawn at the edge of the gorge. I'm not sure how far her ambition reached then. She was hurting over Brett. Then the unimaginable happened, the death of their precious daughter Arkie.

'Anyone else would have been totally defeated, but Wendy turned her gaze outwards with renewed tenacity, and her grief transmuted itself into greater energy still. The result is in the miraculous realm of a child's dream. Strange, each time I visit the mysterious depths and surprises of this garden I feel I am exploring deeper aspects of myself. That's what it does to one.'

Years earlier, Wendy had told Barry how, when she was a child, Frances Hodgson Burnett's book about a secret garden where one could be healed had etched itself into her imagination.

'I may never have gotten to know the extraordinary Wendy Whiteley. Difficult, obsessed, analytical to the point of pain, yet compassionate, humorous and highly intelligent.'

(BARRY)

Through the Eyes of Friends

'"The artist is he who can take a piece of flint and wring out of it drops of attar of roses," is a famous saying by Walter Sickert, the English artist. That's what Wendy has done.'

Barry admits that he too has always had a secret garden. 'Even now, at my home, which has a semi-overgrown, mini-Balinese jungle garden, there is a bower of sunlight for growing herbs. I feel immersed in and protected by it, and that it will look after me and my family if nurtured and loved. This connects me to my childhood, when I lived a solitary life with my mother in Adelaide. I was an only child whose father died, shot down in a Lancaster bomber in Germany when I was nine months old.

'We had a garden in which I grew strawberries, radishes and sweet peas. At the bottom were two ancient fruit trees: one apricot, the other peach, spliced with nectarine.

'In the summer I used to lose myself high up in the peach tree amongst its dense foliage, and I built a cubby-house, or more a platform, from which I could peer above the rooftops, reach out and pick a huge, juicy white peach, crushing it in my mouth. To this day, the smell of peach takes me back to that sanctuary. I used to think, if something happened to my mother, and I had no one, I could stay up in that tree and somehow survive.'

Barry feels that when Wendy is no longer with us, the magical realm of the Lavender Bay Secret Garden will reflect her true soul. 'More than Brett's works,' he maintains. 'More even than Wendy's unmistakable charisma, weaving her story so richly through our own recollections of the twentieth century. We only hope that the people of Sydney will take it upon themselves to preserve Wendy Whiteley's Secret Garden.

'"The artist is he who can take a piece of flint and wring out of it drops of attar of roses," is a famous saying by Walter Sickert, the English artist. That's what Wendy has done.'

Through the Eyes of Friends

188

Made Wijaya, who lives between his homes in Bali and Lavender Bay, favours using his Balinese scythe to get the pruning finesse he desires.

(*MADE*) 'Oddly enough, all Wendy's idiosyncrasies work like a charm. This garden draws you in, in the most friendly, trusting way … It gets full marks as a secret garden – I love it all.'

MADE WIJAYA

A flamboyant extrovert, Made Wijaya, Bali-based landscape designer and scribe extraordinaire, started life in Sydney's eastern suburbs as Michael White.

Having been a schoolboy tennis champion, then a Sydney University architecture student, in 1973, aged twenty, he went to Bali and never left. He studied Balinese architecture, gardens, religion, drama, dance and morphed into Made Wijaya, prime exponent of Bali-style landscaping.

He famously landscaped a garden for rockstar David Bowie on Mustique, and at one point employed five hundred Balinese gardeners on international projects. 'I was credited with inventing 'Bali-style landscaping', though, to my mind, I was introducing the 'Artful Natural' English tropical style, which I so admired in Sydney's Botanic Gardens as a boy,' Made explains.

Made lives in Sanur, Bali, in a relaxed garden compound house. He regularly visits Sydney, staying in his Lavender Bay apartment across the lower Walker Street steps from Wendy's house. He's easy to spot, in his array of batik sarongs and panama hats.

Wendy and Made have been good friends for a long time, and Wendy launched one of his books on Balinese architecture. Theatrical feuds do, however, occur when Made emerges with his Balinese scythes and starts wildly pruning the lush foliage in the garden strip down the centre of the steps.

'I prefer the finesse of the cut I get with a Balinese scythe,' Made explains. 'I use the actions from my tennis-playing years: big forehand and backhand swings, and an overhead volley slice too.'

What Made calls pruning, Wendy calls slashing. 'Sometimes he's like a mad assassin, thrashing away and leaving dead limbs everywhere!' Wendy decries. Her rage rises when Made abandons the cut branches where they fall, 'expecting a team of fifteen gardeners to come and pick it all up, like they do in Bali,' Wendy huffs. She's been known to roar at Made, 'Pick up your damned leaves'. Made will later saunter into Wendy's kitchen to make peace. 'We squabble a lot, but we are actually fond of each other,' he admits.

Made is the full dichotomy. In a most erudite manner, he will expound his immense knowledge of ancient and contemporary Balinese culture – then roll into uproarious gossip, laughing like a frog. Made professes huge admiration for Wendy's Secret Garden, though not without sprinkling through some acid criticisms.

'She used to have a fabulous tapestry of large swathes of colours, but now she's too fine-tuning, so some sections are beginning to look *petit point*,' he groans. 'It's too high-maintenance! And that ring-a-rosie circle of small stepping stones and doughnut of violets around the Bangalow palms is *wrong* Wendy, *wrong*. The garden snobs will mark you *down* Wendy.

'Yet oddly enough,' he adds, face glowing with pleasure, 'all her idiosyncrasies work like a charm. This garden draws you in, in the most friendly, trusting way, so you want to keep on discovering more of its quirkiness. It gets full marks as a secret garden, I love it all.'

'I prefer the finesse of the cut I get with a Balinese scythe. I use the actions from my tennis-playing years: big forehand and backhand swings, and an overhead volley slice too.'

(*MADE*)

Through the Eyes of Friends

Monstera deliciosa in flower.

(**WW**) 'I love the flower of the
Monstera deliciosa. It is so beautiful
– nature at its best. It reminds me of
Robert Mapplethorpe's photographs.'

Made with local resident and bush
regeneration enthusiast, Jan Cork.

'Its quirkiness is an extension of Wendy's personality – a mixture of rustic and high style, the haiku and the high Zen.'

(MADE)

Made met Brett and Wendy in the early seventies. 'I came to parties in their Lavender Bay house soon after they moved in here,' Made recalls. 'I was intrigued with the haute bohemian art set. Brett was the starry oracle, Wendy the goddess with incredible style. She had a magician's touch – she'd arrange a bowl of flowers and a few objects of furniture and bring the whole room to life. She's a fabulous dancer and we were all knocked out by her beauty.

'Both were searingly intelligent; so spirited and cantankerous. They argued magnificently at times. I got to know Brett and Wendy better in 1979, when they first came to Bali and I took them around to temple festivals. Then they all came up in 1980 with Joel Elenberg when Joel's cancer was terminal, so he could pass away in Bali.'

Made remembers the overgrown landfill site in front of the Whiteley house as 'the Badlands; a dangerous zone, a hangout for vagabonds and rats.'

The wide nature strip that runs down the centre of the lower Walker Street steps was also something of a bleak wasteland, mainly large fig trees and weeds. In the eighties, in an early attempt at beautification, local residents got together to plant the strip with sub-tropical foliage under the trees.

Wendy was a keen helper, but remarks that Brett archly declined, saying he'd rather be painting and pay someone to do his share.

Although Wendy and her gardeners are among those who help look after the Walker Street steps garden, it's not part of the Secret Garden, so Made regards this strip as his territory to prune, in his mode.

'Laypeople often freak out when I start pruning with scythes and machetes, but you must prune gardens quite savagely to allow light and air in,' Made maintains.

If he were writing a critique, Made explains that he'd call the Walker Street steps garden, and much of Wendy's Secret Garden, Sub-tropical Artful Natural.

'Artful Natural is the English natural landscape movement … God's the best gardener, so try to create a natural look as if God did it,' he elaborates.

'Sub-tropical Artful Natural is more of a lush, ordered jungle. You plant palms, tree ferns, bird's nest ferns, bamboo, aspidistras and lilies, all the things that look great with huge fig trees. But there's a very fine line between ordered jungle and a mess. You don't want the mixed salad look. You must keep the shapes but not let it look too blended.'

When Wendy started making the Secret Garden, Made says he offered suggestions, 'and got snapped at'. He adds, 'Over the years I've suggested *less* plant variety, and *more* pruning, and been ignored!'

As we step into the Secret Garden, Made says, with a mixture of exasperation and admiration, 'In professional landscaping terms, Wendy breaks all the rules. With a small garden you can have lots of variety, but as a garden vista gets bigger, you should utilise more massing and less variety. Too much detail gets messy.'

He would have cleared the entire site first, seen the bones, and then decided on a design.

(**WW**) 'Some flowers smile, others look pensive or shy. Others show off, or brazenly flirt.'

'That's how a professional would have approached it, although the result too often can look overly ordered and contrived,' Made laments.

Whereas Wendy did it like a mélange – clearing, stabilising, sculpting, planting, and then sewing it all together. It happened by trial and error, rather than any grand plan.

'The Secret Garden is huge, but it's all done on the scale of a domestic garden, so it doesn't feel like a public garden,' Made continues.

'Its quirkiness is an extension of Wendy's personality – a mixture of rustic and high style, the haiku and the high Zen. It has a slightly olde worlde ambience, a little bit Victorian, a bit rustic with the mounted found objects. Like everything Wendy does, it's sensual and mixed with high-end modern stuff like the Whiteley and Elenberg sculptures. She is so stylish in her combinations of colour, then splashes of colour, and unexpected combinations of textures and shapes.

'This is no amateur hand dabbling at a spot of gardening here, it's *too good*. You know you're looking at an artistic masterpiece … all the more enchanting as you ponder, how on earth could this Secret Garden be here?'

Made praises Wendy for her cleverness at minimising the impact of garden hardscape, such as paths, handrails and steps and maximising the garden softscape – the planting. 'There's no defined hardscape, no parallel lines, no edges. The paths and handrails wind organically, and the handrails are slim gnarled branches,' he elaborates.

'So often municipal gardens are ruined by regulation park furniture, and Wendy's avoided this with her pre-loved domestic outdoor furniture, tables with umbrellas, and poetic benches. Though, ignoring the dictum that "less is more", she keeps adding more table and chair settings and more plants!'

Ambling along, Made gestures, 'Here's a bank of bird's nest ferns, orange-flowering clivias, a cycad, all speared with sculptural tree ferns above. Very happy with this! But to my eye, you don't need to add the lady finger palm, spider lilies, flax, a standard grevillea and a loquat tree. But here's the allure, it's got something for all tastes and all seasons. And she's such a stunning stylist, in the house and in the garden, that it never feels cluttered.'

Up above in a tall coral tree, rainbow lorikeets with their vivid plumage of blue, green and orange are noisily feasting on nectar from the red, claw-shaped flowers.

Gazing up, Made remarks, 'The birds and bees know their job is to help nature procreate. Flowers are broadcasting, "Here I am, ripe and ready for pollinating". Gardens are so sexual. Look at the *Monstera deliciosa* fruit showing off their phallic sizes, boasting "I'm bigger than you are", worse than a schoolboys' locker room.'

He pauses nostalgically at a tall stand of shell ginger. 'Good gardeners always bring cuttings from friends' gardens, and I brought this shell ginger from the historic Bronte House garden when our friends, Peter and Carole Muller, lived there. Wendy's now propagated numerous clumps from the original one. See how the flower heads resemble clusters of small creamy pink-yellow shells. Some of Wendy's daturas also came from Bronte House.'

'*Gardens are so sexual. Look at the* Monstera deliciosa *fruit showing off their phallic sizes, boasting "I'm bigger than you are", worse than a schoolboys' locker room.*'

(*MADE*)

'If you see kids running through a garden and having fun, then you know it's a success.'

(*MADE*)

Three young children romp through the garden ahead of us, a look of wonder on their faces as they stop at the ancient scooter mounted on a plinth, then see racks of aged metal milk cans and billies. Others scamper around, trying to spot the clues in a treasure hunt.

'You could easily imagine pixies living amongst all this,' Made says, grinning. 'If you see kids running through a garden and having fun, then you know it's a success.'

Made reminisces about his own childhood secret garden. 'It was a piece of coastal bush on the walk from Bondi to Tamarama, where Sculpture by the Sea is now staged. I called it my pixie glen, and I believed pixies lived there, so did all the local kids. I was in awe of the place; it was very special in my imagination.'

A few months later, Made is back in Sydney to give a lecture, staying with Wendy as his own apartment is full of guests.

'Wendy's gone to a wedding lunch; she went off dressed like a magnificent character from *The Mikado*. So I thought I'd hop out and do a spot of pruning,' he stage whispers. 'Fast growing sub-tropical plants get very messy and need lots of pruning.'

Late afternoon, when Wendy's returned home, we all sit on the balcony with a pot of tea and homemade passionfruit cake. Made expounds, 'Wendy and I are both autodidacts, self-taught gardeners. We both have a passionate interest in creating spaces. One difference is that Wendy's such a plant-lover that she overplants and is too reluctant to prune – whereas I'm happy to get in and hack away when needed.'

Wendy concedes, 'Look, I now realise that we planted trees and bushes too close together, so one plant grows sideways, struggling to reach the light, and we have to prop it up. I did find it very hard to prune a tree I'd grown from birth.

'But I'm now becoming a strong believer in opening up sight lines and windows through the garden foliage, so you can see through a section.

'I particularly want more sight lines through the taller foliage, so you can see the harbour and the Bridge and be reminded where you are. So I might finally become an enthusiastic pruner.'

Made pours more tea and concludes, 'You could take away half the planting here, and it would have more majesty – but then it wouldn't have the unique quirkiness of Wendy's Secret Garden.'

Two very different passionate gardeners, top professional Paul Bangay and self-taught amateur Wendy, enjoy an instant connection on their first meeting.

(*WW*) 'He was lovely – I really liked him. I hope he comes back.'

(*PAUL*) 'What's fabulous about this big garden is that it doesn't look like a professional landscape designer's garden. I love it all the more for this … It's absolutely unique; I'm thrilled by it.'

PAUL BANGAY

For quite some time, Wendy had been hearing that Paul Bangay, the Melbourne-based prince of elegant, classical landscape design, wanted to visit the Secret Garden.

She was mystified by this, as Bangay's stately gardens, with their master-planned geometric perfection, clipped box hedges, immaculately coiffed rows of trees, emerald green lawns, formal paving and serene pools, seemed a world apart from the Secret Garden.

'He'll probably hate it here – there's not a parterre or avenue of pleached pears to be seen!' Wendy remarks, her clear blue eyes rolling heavenwards. 'And most certainly not a tightly knitted, flawless English box hedge!'

Finally, a visit is arranged. Wendy suggests that Paul arrive early and she'll walk him around the garden, followed by lunch on the balcony, overlooking it all.

Corrado is cajoled into cooking posh pizzas, and they are indeed posh: a degustation of pizzas with lobster, prawns, squid and squid ink, goat's cheese, fresh herbs and greens from the garden.

'Mr Bangay will be used to all those upper-crust clients, so we'd better turn it on,' Wendy notes merrily. She gets dressed up, wraps her hair in a batik turban, and the doorbell rings.

In bounds this enthusiastic, super-fit character in a blue T-shirt and work pants, a boyish grin on a handsome face, eyes as blue as hers. Within moments Paul Bangay has hugged Wendy, begun a down-to-earth conversation laced with racy good humour, and the two have bonded like twin souls.

They head out eagerly towards the Secret Garden. Pausing at the top of the entry steps, beneath the Moreton Bay fig tree, contemplating what lies ahead, Paul rubs his hands together, expressing a first thought, 'I hate it when you can see the whole garden in one glance. A successful garden relies on intrigue, to beckon you through with a sense of anticipation. I'm already being powerfully beckoned'.

Pacing down the stairs into the first grassy enclosure, he spins around and says, 'I love the sensation of a walled garden here; I love the feeling of wrapping yourself in a big blanket of trees and foliage and shutting out the outside world.'

Wendy looks pleased, and explains that most of the Secret Garden is a virtual walled garden.

Paul walks on, exclaiming, 'I'm relishing the intimate feeling of being hugged by this garden. You're in your own little paradise'.

He detours up steps, along paths covered in leafy canopies. 'How do you get bird's nest ferns to grow so immense? And look at the number of flowers crammed on that *Brugmansia*, you can barely see a leaf.'

Wendy retorts, 'I still call them daturas.'

Paul, 'The name changed.'

Wendy, 'I don't care!'

'I hate it when you can see the whole garden in one glance. A successful garden relies on intrigue, to beckon you through with a sense of anticipation. I'm already being powerfully beckoned'.

(*PAUL*)

Through the Eyes of Friends

(**WW**) 'I don't want a garden restricted by tight corsets of prim, clipped box hedges. I want the opposite — voluptuous plantings spilling over the edges.'

'I love the fact that so many people are using this garden. It makes me sad that so many large, expensive private gardens are created around large homes, and no one ever goes into those gardens and uses them.'

(*PAUL*)

They come upon a mulberry tree, with its top pruned off so it will grow like a weeping umbrella, allowing the fruit to be picked. It was too high to reach, Wendy explains.

'Great work,' Paul endorses. 'Mulberry trees are coming back into fashion, people want them again, as fewer houses use washing lines, and dryers have taken over. So the old curse of mulberry diarrhoea from birds' droppings all over your washing has joined a bygone era.'

The agapanthus are nodding full pompom heads of blue flowers, and Paul's eyes are darting everywhere: up, down, sideways, backwards, enjoying the surprises and moments of Wendy whimsy.

Midway through he stops and declares, 'What's fabulous about this big garden is that it doesn't look like a professional landscape designer's garden. I love it all the more for this. It hasn't got that over-designed look. It's absolutely unique; I'm thrilled by it.'

'It's not *too untidy* for your eye?' Wendy quizzes.

'On the contrary,' Paul responds. 'I always used to be so passionate about formality in gardens; straight lines, geometry and symmetry. Mass-planting. As I'm maturing, I'm changing. I'm enjoying mixing some informality with the formality. I'm softening my planting scheme, so I might now put a mixture of blowsy, flowering perennials alongside a clipped box hedge. I'm adding more curvaceous lines and greater diversity of species ... aiming to weave a tapestry of colours like the Oriental rug effect you capture.'

Back at the house, Paul leans on the balcony rail with a glass of wine, surveying the garden stretching below, the harbour, the last of the falling jacaranda blooms.

'You know, I never could have done this,' he states. 'I'm so used to clearing the entire site first, drawing up a master plan, bringing in the bulldozers and big machines to sculpt and pour concrete and then setting out all the trees and shrubs to plant.'

'I would have loved a bulldozer and big machines at times too,' Wendy concedes, 'but it was impossible on this site. We had to do it all by hand, incrementally.'

Over lunch, great gardens of the world are discussed and dissected, Paul declaring, 'Aren't we so lucky to have a burning passion for gardening? It adds so much to your life'.

He keeps an eye on the numbers walking into the Secret Garden, and remarks, 'I love the fact that so many people are using this garden. It makes me sad that so many large, expensive private gardens are created around large homes, and no one ever goes into those gardens and uses them.'

As he's leaving, I ask Paul Bangay if he thinks Wendy has achieved garden Nirvana.

'Absolutely, yes,' he beams.

Wendy looks pleased, and after he's left she adds her own postscript.

'A lot of landscape gardeners have come here, and most, like Paul, have been positive. Only a few walk around with spectacles and pinched noses, muttering that I shouldn't be planting XYZ here because it's *not native*. I reply, "This never was native bush, it's all landfill. So instead of standing here giving me advice, why don't you go and find a piece of land smothered in weeds and rubbish, clean it out and you plant a native garden for the people? Go for it!"'

Through the Eyes of Friends

Wendy and her close friend Helen Simons, at Helen's birthday party.

(*HELEN*) 'The Secret Garden has been an amazing journey, for Wendy and for all of her friends … It's been therapeutic in a way, a catharsis … At the same time, it's been an outlet to push her own creative boundaries, use her exceptional range of skills in bold and sensitive ways.'

HELEN SIMONS

On New Year's Eve, Wendy holds a private party, and a core group of long-time close friends are always on hand to help. Helen Simons, big in spirit, voice and body, is usually near the door, radiating a generous smile and hug, as guests are buzzed in via the security systems. Wonderful melodies will be playing as you walk inside, as Helen is music maestro for the night. Jazz, Latin, soul, Cajun, swing, blues, gospel, flamenco, Queens of New Orleans will be rolling out from her inventive playlist. Helen is usually first to start dancing later in the evening, and will soon have Wendy joining in.

Helen's passion for music gradually supplanted her earlier career in higher education. She was a lecturer in special education in the Faculty of Education at the University of Sydney, recognised for her innovative work with special needs students and teacher training. Alongside this she worked as an FM radio co-host on music shows, an events DJ and organiser, and produced documentary films.

A warm, supportive friend, she's there like a calm rock beside Wendy, forever ready to help when needed. It says a lot about Wendy that she has this circle of trusted, long-time friends; but it is reciprocal, as Wendy is a very true friend herself.

'The Secret Garden has been an amazing journey, for Wendy, and for all of her friends who've watched it happen,' says Helen. 'It's been therapeutic in a way, a catharsis, somewhere she could go to have her own private thoughts and release her frustrations. They're all down in the garden with her, all their ashes – Brett, Arkie, her mother, her father, her beloved dogs. At the same time, it's been an outlet to push her own creative boundaries, use her exceptional range of skills in bold and sensitive ways, and make something beautiful for everyone to see and share.

'Wendy is a very rare person. She's indomitable. No matter what hits her, she gets on with life, and all her pain and emotional problems get buried in the dirt and turned into something glorious. She has an amazing appetite for life.

'Wendy has always been a very self-contained person, but she's become a lot more self-confident and independent in the last decade; she's busy and happy.'

Helen sees a musicality in the Secret Garden's design, a rhythm in its textures, and observes that Wendy's garden opus could be likened to the opus of a jazz improviser or classical composer.

'Wendy's emotional depth and artistic knowledge have led her gardening band in various directions across the landscape,' says Helen, 'with little compositions everywhere finally merging into her own masterpiece. On any day, Wendy as the solo player is digging into the ground, weeding, pulling, planting, lifting and hosing to the sounds of kookaburras, rainbow lorikeets, seagulls and new arrivals, a pair of brush turkeys.

'When you can't find Wendy in the house she's usually disappeared into the garden, and that's it for the rest of the day. When the sun goes down and she is satisfied and physically

'Wendy's emotional depth and artistic knowledge have led her gardening band in various directions across the landscape, with little compositions everywhere finally merging into her own masterpiece.'

(*HELEN*)

Through the Eyes of Friends

> *'In this beautiful setting, I hear the great Australian improvisers taking elements from the classic standards, with a hint of the odd melody line across the pathways.'*
>
> (HELEN)

exhausted, covered in mud with twigs hanging out of her headscarf and the hose is turned off ... her part is done.'

Continuing her musical metaphor, Helen sees the garden shed as housing the gardeners' instruments. 'Sometimes Wendy's band becomes a trio or a quartet, or even a small ensemble when volunteer gardeners join Ruben, Corrado, Jay Jay and Klara and jam happily away.

'In this beautiful setting, I hear the great Australian improvisers taking elements from the classic standards, with a hint of the odd melody line across the pathways. When Wendy the bandleader points her long conductor's finger, the gardeners tune in for directions ... what's next? Each adds their own tune to the garden beds, sometimes in harmony, sometimes in a reluctant struggle for pragmatism.

'The symphonic sounds of the bird life in this glorious, ever-changing creation are sometimes interrupted by the percussion notes of lawnmower, axe or chainsaw, when a dead tree has to come down. Then it's over, and peace and quiet returns to the garden with a gentle melody into the night. Life and death, love, friendship, mirth and celebration have all found their place.

'Brett painted large-scale pictures like *Alchemy*, but this is Wendy's response, still steeped in the conversation. Is it any wonder that Wendy's Secret Garden is no longer a secret, but a cherished community destination for locals and international visitors?'

———

If guests arrive early on New Year's Eve, it's likely that Wendy will still be upstairs in her bedroom, in the shower and deciding what to wear, running late as she couldn't stop herself from working on something she wanted to finish in the garden. There's always extra precautionary work to do to prepare the Secret Garden to cope with the deluge of revellers who gather around Sydney Harbour foreshores to watch the fireworks.

Gary will have been in the kitchen for hours, patiently peeling prawns. Wendy will likely make some tantalising dish, like black pasta with seafood, and inventive salads.

Poet Robert Adamson usually arrives with his homemade fruit cake, baking being a skill he acquired in his younger life as a pastry chef; his wife, photographer Juno Gemes, will be with him, keen to enjoy the evening.

Anna Schwartz is usually present, along with her husband, publisher and businessman Morry Schwartz. Made Wijaya will make a theatrical entrance, garbed in a celebratory Balinese sarong and hat. Peter Kingston will pop over from his house next door, where he'll have his own party in full swing.

Artist Michael Johnson will be sitting with the smokers on the balcony, waxing lyrical about nature. His wife, Margo, will be opening and offering around the French champagne she's brought. Wendy is a teetotaller, but happy for others to enjoy a drink.

New Year's Eve revellers spill over into the Secret Garden, and Wendy and her gardeners pray not to find too much damage next morning.

As evening falls, Clark Park will be crammed with people sitting on rugs, with assorted bags of food and beverages (alcohol is officially banned); more will be spilling into the Secret Garden, and Wendy and her gardeners will be praying that not too many plants get trampled, and no handrails or furniture get broken as the night's revelries step up. If Wendy catches anyone in the act of vandalism, she hurls them a blistering lecture they'll never forget.

As midnight approaches, anticipation about this year's fireworks extravaganza builds. It's no longer possible to watch the Sydney Harbour fireworks from the balcony, as the Moreton Bay fig is now so large it blocks the view, so Wendy and her guests go down to a small section of grass under the Moreton Bay fig, where she tries to reserve a spot.

Last year, at around 11 p.m. as the party continued up in the house, I found Wendy sitting alone in this spot, staring into the darkness. She looked suddenly so alone.

So many thoughts must have been swirling in her head. So much of her life has been tied up with this place: her younger self, and now her older self. Will she ever fully comprehend it all? Friends soon join her and midnight comes. Fireworks burst over the harbour. Lavender Bay is filled with revellers, cheering and chorusing, 'Happy New Year'.

Next morning, as usual, Wendy is down with her gardeners, assessing the damage and cleaning up the mess and rubbish left behind. They anticipate some trampled plants, but hope for no broken handrails or smashed chairs. Sadly, they do sometimes find the latter.

As usual, most bystanders assume that the council, the government, or someone else is paying the gardeners to collect the rubbish and fix the damage. Not so. Wendy has paid for everything right from the start, and, at the time of writing, she still pays for everything.

I've witnessed this scenario countless times. Wendy will be working in the garden. A visitor stops beside her, and queries, 'So does the council pay for all this?'

Wendy: 'No.'

Visitor: 'So are you a volunteer?'

Wendy: 'No. I'm just the mad woman who made this garden.'

Visitor, persisting: 'Oh, then who pays you?'

Wendy: 'No one pays me. I just do it because it seemed like a good idea.'

'I'm just the mad woman who made this garden.'

(WW)

CHAPTER 8

The Whiteley House at Lavender Bay

Brett Whiteley
Interior, Lavender Bay, 1974
Ink on cardboard, 88 cm x 75 cm
Photo: Christies' Images Ltd
© Wendy Whiteley

(**WW**) 'When we bought the house in 1974, the interior was two storeys of dingy flats, with no linking staircases. The exterior was spat-out concrete stucco and liver bricks. We knocked off the hideous stucco, cement-bagged the entire exterior and painted it.

'Then we built the tower, with a spiral staircase inside to link the storeys. Initially the tower was topped with a straw thatch roof somewhat like Monet's haystacks, but the parrots had a ball stealing all the straw, so we replaced it with cedar shingles.

'In major renovations in 2007 I gained two extra storeys. I raised the attic roof, put in the dormer window and skylights to open up the main bedroom, then excavated the basement for the gardeners room and much-needed storage.'

W hen the Whiteleys moved into Lavender Bay in 1969, it was a very different house from today's immaculate four-storey dwelling, with its Rapunzel tower enclosing a bespoke stainless steel and glass elevator. Nor then had the earlier, down-at-heel area been gentrified.

'The bones of the house are still the same,' Wendy explains, 'but almost every centimetre of the house has been extensively renovated in the years since.

'If it hadn't been for the harbour view and the fabulous natural light in Lavender Bay, we never would have stayed in this house,' she continues.

'There's not enough room for a painter like Brett to work here. We'd always had our home and studio combined. Brett liked to work at all hours; literally wake up and walk five paces to a painting. He tended to paint from where he was, using the subject matter at hand. I was often the subject matter, and sometimes he painted himself. He'd paint what was going on around him, so often it was the room as I'd arranged it, with me as the model – in the bath, on a sofa, or wherever. Not that I was lying around naked on one hip all the time!'

In 1969, the 1907 Federation house, built in brick on locally quarried sandstone block footings, had been divided into two flats on two levels, with no linking staircase. The Whiteleys rented the upper floor, and their artist friend Rollin Schlicht rented downstairs.

'Arkie was just five, and we squashed ourselves into that one level. At the front was a sitting room which Brett used as his studio, then another room, which became our bedroom. Arkie's bedroom was tucked into a corner, then we had a small kitchen and bathroom. It was very dark, gloomy and rundown, so we painted all the walls white. We'd done that in other places we'd rented too.'

The balcony, then only narrow and flush with the exterior house walls, was shoddily enclosed with fibro, rotting and unsafe.

'We fixed a piece of chicken wire across the balcony opening, and turned it into an aviary, as it was unusable for anything else,' Wendy continues.

'We had pigeons and white fantail doves; then they all started breeding with the park pigeons and we ended up with a motley crew. Brett made some drawings of them, fantails mixed with park pigeons, long feathers growing on their feet. We also rescued some limping peewees with broken wings. The cat would occasionally bring home a bird too, so we'd grab it and put it in the aviary as well.

'We had some parrots, but they started eating all the aviary plants, so the parrots were evicted!

'In New York, when we lived on the rooftop of the Chelsea Hotel, we had an aviary and some mad exotic birds that flew around the apartment. They'd escape, and Brett would be running down the street trying to catch them. We had little ducklings that someone gave Arkie at the Chelsea too; they grew into huge adult ducks which squawked like guard dogs.

'We always had a bit of a menagerie, including several much-loved dogs. This is the first time in my life that I haven't had a dog, after they all grew old and died.

'We'd always had our home and studio combined. Brett liked to work at all hours; to literally wake up and walk five paces to a painting.'

(**WW**)

The Whiteley House at Lavender Bay

(**WW**) 'The interior was depressingly dark and pokey, divided into many small rooms, with ghastly stained glass windows blocking out the light and views.

'We wanted to open the house up, so one night during a party a friend started bashing down the sitting room wall. Then Brett phoned an architect friend who came racing down. His face went white as he yelled, "*Stop*, the house will collapse, this is a supporting wall!"

'We'd been in Majorca and loved the Spanish influence of arches, so we proceeded to knock out walls correctly, and reinforce the opening arches with steel.

'We stripped mouldy wallpaper off remaining walls, painted everything white; ripped up cack-brown lino, sanded the floor and painted it with marine varnish. Unfortunately the timber yellowed with so much light flooding in, so later on I limed the floor white.'

The Whiteley House
at Lavender Bay

(**WW**) 'Many of Brett's gorgeous Lavender Bay paintings show the main balcony with a Matisse-like double scroll metal balustrade. It was Brett's poetic licence to paint this classic French railing, because the main balcony off the sitting room never had such an ornate balustrade, only a simple railing.

'So when I added a balcony off the main bedroom in my last renovations, as a tribute to Brett, I added the Matissean double scroll balustrade that he'd always imagined.'

> *'This guy started attacking the wall with a sledgehammer, and a few others joined in.'*
>
> (WW)

'We had a fox once, which I bought at Paddy's Markets, at Brett's insistence. It slept on Arkie's bed, then one day the fox pissed off, looking for a mate. I feel a bit guilty about that.

'We had bantams and a rooster down amidst the brambles on the vacant railway land, where the garden is now. The rooster would crow loudly at 3 a.m., then a man with a raucous American accent would ring us up and roar down the phone, "COCK-A-DOODLE-DOO!!!" to make sure we'd been woken up as well.

'Kingo next door had some chooks in a cage down there for a while too, but the poor rooster and chooks eventually died or got taken when dogs or foxes broke into their cage.

'The railway arch down below was full of homeless people for years,' remembers Wendy. 'A woman called Priscilla used to light up her boyfriend's mattress if they'd had a fight, so the fire brigade had to come in. Priscilla would be yelling up to me, "Call the police, Mrs Whiteley!"'

In 1974 the Whiteleys bought the house. It was the first time they'd ever owned a property, and it marked the end of their gypsy lives of the previous decade.

'One night we were having a party, and people drank a bit too much, and one guy was a renovator,' Wendy recalls. 'We said, "The first thing that's got to go is the interior brick wall that divides up the front part of the house". We wanted more space and more light coming in. So this guy started attacking the wall with a sledgehammer, and a few others joined in. Then Brett went, "*Jesus, the whole house might fall down!*" so we rang an architect friend who hot-footed over and said, "*Stop!*", informing us that we needed a steel beam across the ceiling because this was a supporting wall.

'Brett and I had a lot of parties here, more a bohemian crowd at first. Then it became the rounds of entertaining gallery directors, curators, clients who want to meet you, and friends from across the creative arts. A lot of rowdy and argumentative behaviour went on, and great discussions about art and life. I'm a good cook, so I always put on a generous spread of food.'

Next, the aviary was farewelled and the balcony was opened up and extended out 2 metres from the house facade to transform it into an open-air balcony.

'In 1974 we had a clear view of the harbour,' Wendy explains. 'The Moreton Bay fig tree didn't even reach the top of the balcony, and we could see straight down to the three cabbage tree palms beside Lavender Bay jetty. Brett loved painting them, in numerous guises. Brett painted trees that weren't there too, like a sumptuously flowering jacaranda and a plum tree, but that's his poetic licence. Now all the fig trees are taller and screen the view, almost obscuring the three cabbage tree palms.'

Then the tower went up, and the house's exterior brick walls were bagged and painted cream.

Wendy sometimes hears passers-by outside her house, staring up at the tower and exclaiming, 'Oh look at that – it must be an old lighthouse!'

'Brett always wanted a storybook tower,' Wendy explains. 'He'd painted a house with a tower on the end panel of *The American Dream*. It was a symbol of paradise, somewhere to live that was calm and beautiful.

'It was a helluva job to put the tower in. We had to excavate right down to bedrock, but the tower actually served a functional purpose, as we put a spiral staircase inside it linking all levels of the house, including inside the attic roof space which became the main bedroom.

'Brett wanted a dip pool outside, so we built one; it's 3 metres deep but doesn't get any sun, so it's heated. We put a tea-tree fence up around the house block, which hides the dip pool.'

When Brett died in 1992, friends counselled Wendy to sell the house and start again.

'I thought about changing my name back to Wendy Julius and moving, but you don't really start again. Things change, but your past is part of your life. I loved Lavender Bay, it was my heart and soul place, and I wanted to keep the house for Arkie. When I started making the garden it made even more sense to stay and fix something up, that I could fix up.

'At first I thought I was doing the garden for Arkie, and she loved it. I thought Arkie would keep on looking after the garden and ensure that it was given to the public. When Arkie died in 2001, I knew I'd stay here forever, holding onto every precious memory we shared.'

After Arkie died, her two pet dachshunds, Mrs Peaches and Colonel Duffer, came to live at Lavender Bay with Wendy and her two dogs, Owl Feathers and Madame Mao. Four small dogs were now scampering around Wendy's heels; their company was comforting.

'Brett and I had always had two dogs, everywhere we'd lived,' says Wendy. 'When Arkie moved to London, she got two dogs of her own, Mrs Peaches and Colonel Duffer, and brought them back to Australia when she returned to live here, at Palm Beach.'

Booga and Bag were the first dogs to join the Whiteley household when Brett, Wendy and five-year-old Arkie moved into Lavender Bay.

'Booga was a dachshund cross; I bought him at Paddy's Markets, and Brett and Joel Elenberg fell about laughing, saying that he was the ugliest dog they'd ever seen. Brett called him Booga, after a character in a Frankenstein movie. Then Brett became totally obsessed with Booga, but unfortunately Booga went out hunting for a lady mate and was run over in traffic.

'Bag was the progeny of my mother's Yorkshire terrier and a mutty, feathery dog that lived across the road from her. Sadly, Bag was stolen. The next pair of dogs we had were Sense and Reason. Sense was a dachshund cross, and Reason came from another litter of my mother's Yorkshire terrier and the mutt across the road.'

Sense and Reason both died of old age while Wendy spent a year away in a London rehabilitation clinic.

'When I came home in late 1987, Arkie asked, "Mum, are you going to get another dog?" I replied that the only dog I really wanted was a Maltese-silky cross. So Arkie looked in the newspaper and found one, then drove out to the breeder's place and came home with Owl Feathers.

'A year later I got Madame Mao. She was a black and white shih tzu, a Chinese lion dog with a flat face, long droopy ears, large dark eyes, and long silky hair that dragged over the ground unless you cut it.

'Brett always wanted a storybook tower. He'd painted a house with a tower on the end panel of The American Dream. *It was a symbol of paradise, somewhere to live that was calm and beautiful.'*

(**WW**)

The Whiteley House at Lavender Bay

(**WW**) 'Arkie with Owl Feathers, Mrs Peaches, Madam Mao and Colonel Duffer.'

'I always looked after the interiors of all our homes. Brett liked and admired the way I created interiors, including the "tablescapes", so he was very happy that I was always around to do this.'

(**WW**)

'I got Madame Mao from the pound. She'd been shaved because she'd been wandering around the streets and her hair was in a terrible knotted state. She looked like E.T. (the extra-terrestrial in the Steven Spielberg sci-fi film).

'I said, "If nobody claims this dog, I want her". They rang and said she was mine. Madame Mao was divine, absolutely devoted to me. She grew this beautiful long drapery of hair, but it became full of sticks on her walks, so after a while I got her a very smart hairdo from the dog groomers' salon.'

Wendy admits that her dogs were always thoroughly pampered, fed on freshly poached chicken and vegetables, or freshly cooked beef and vegetables.

The four small dogs all died, one by one. Mrs Peaches and Owl Feathers were the last two left, then Mrs Peaches died, and finally Owl Feathers, aged twenty.

'I might get more dogs, but I seem to have been so busy with other things,' Wendy remarks.

Around 2006, Wendy discovered termites attacking parts of the house, and there were warnings that the sandstone footings might move, as they'd done in old houses nearby, so it was time for serious renovations and underpinning.

As usual with Wendy, once she's on a project, there's no stopping her. Everything was done to perfection, with Wendy obsessively hovering over architects, engineers, builders and tradesmen. She decided to flood the house with as much natural light as possible, so glass roofs and skylights went in over the large kitchen and back sections of the house. The main bedroom ceiling was raised to enlarge the space, and glass galore went in. Silvery zinc sheets replaced old dark sections of roof.

'Looking ahead to my dotage years, when I might be unable to manage stairs, I was persuaded to replace the staircase with an elevator inside the tower,' Wendy explains. 'It was a helluva job getting the elevator custom-designed and built, but it works.'

Wendy decided to dig out the ample under-the-house space inside the high sandstone footings, and convert it into a usable basement level, with a gardeners' room, kitchen, bathroom, and storage rooms for her numerous files and archives. The basement's new limestone floor has underfloor heating.

'Before, we just had a ladder going to this under-the-house space, and we used it for storage. An art student lived down there like a wombat for about six months when we first had the house, as she had nowhere else to live and she seemed to like it. The things we do when we're young …' Wendy reminisces.

The house renovations were so major that Wendy moved out and lived nearby in a rented studio/boatshed on Lavender Bay. Each morning she'd walk across from the boatshed to work in the Secret Garden, and also to deal with the inevitable dramas and delays of home renovations. I remember witnessing Wendy conduct embattled discussions about her preferred method of liming new kitchen cupboard doors, and debating the correct colour tone of marble flooring on a lower level.

*The Whiteley House
at Lavender Bay*

214

(**WW**) 'A rare sight, my zinc kitchen-dining table, with a clear top! Usually it has compost heaps of paperwork growing as I try to deal with it all. I like working at the kitchen table, it's near the front door and I'm more in the centre of everything that's happening, people coming and going. It's a friendly room, filled with light. I probably overdid the light with a huge skylight, which gets so hot in summer I had to add a louvre shade cover.'

After I'd been watching the progress of the Secret Garden for several years, in 2006 Wendy agreed that I could write the first major story to be published about the garden. There was always a fear that if the garden was publicised too soon, it might be stopped. She thought it better to wait till the Secret Garden was more established, then hopefully its own strength would help to preserve it.

That year, Wendy showed me a large crate of very personal letters, cards and photographs that visitors to the Secret Garden had sent her, with heartfelt handwritten messages. A primary school class had made a whole album of drawings and little stories about the garden.

That first large crate of letters has since grown to umpteen large crates of letters, photographs, signed visitors' books, council and heritage documents and Secret Garden memorabilia.

The renovations were finally completed in 2007, with the house acquiring four levels, all designed to be extremely functional.

One room Wendy now spends a lot of time in is her new enlarged kitchen-dining room. It's a gorgeous high-ceilinged kitchen, more like an art gallery, with everything pleasing to the eye.

Dozens of large, collector's-item blue and white ceramic bowls, dishes and vases sit atop the tall, limed wooden cupboards. Stacks of blue and white serving plates rest on open shelves, including a dozen designed by Wendy's friend Lin Utzon.

Wendy's old faithful aluminium Atomic coffee percolators, which sat permanently on her stainless steel stove and were used daily, have now been retired. Coffee afficionados revered the Italian-designed Atomic, which achieved cult status.

'I love its rounded sculptural shape, and it makes great coffee,' says Wendy, 'but mine were so old and over-used that parts kept breaking and were too hard to replace.' A modern, stainless steel coffee machine now sits on the white marble benchtop.

On the island in the centre of the kitchen, a Balinese carved wooden stand is always laden with organic fruit, which Keny buys from a trusted supplier. Loaves of interesting bread and a cake or biscuits usually sit beside the fruit stand, ready to feed the constant flow of droppers-in. In front of a large window, rows of Cuban lolly jars line up, filled with various pastas, lentils and grains. Several of Brett's hand-painted pottery vases grace the shelves.

'I've never really had a dining room before,' Wendy remarks. 'I'd do occasional formal dinners with ten people seated at that big heavy seventeenth century oak table that's pushed against the wall in the sitting room. But it's so heavy to move it's painful. Now that I have a dining room nook and a smaller dining table in this sunny part of the kitchen, I love it and use it constantly. I found this oval dining table in the street, and had it zinc-coated. I've put in zinc skirting boards too. I love the tone of zinc, it's softer than stainless steel.'

Though Wendy has a separate large office on the next level down, the zinc dining table in the kitchen nook soon became house headquarters. Piles of papers, messages, invitations, requests for her help and opinions on art-related matters mount up on the table and are pushed aside to make space for a quick meal.

'I found this oval dining table in the street, and had it zinc-coated. I've put in zinc skirting boards too. I love the tone of zinc, it's softer than stainless steel.'

(**WW**)

*The Whiteley House
at Lavender Bay*

ABOVE (*WW*) 'Janet Hawley and me sharing a moment of happy relief when, after two years of working on this book, the pages are almost ready to go off to the printers. We've been friends a long time, and always able to wend our way through the sometimes difficult and emotional landscape of life. We both share a real hope for the future, and a belief that the making of things beautiful,

be it paintings, gardens or architecture, and sharing this with friends and family, is the true meaning of life.'

OPPOSITE (*WW*) 'Brett wanted a swimming pool outside before I was allowed to put in a new kitchen. It's a very practical kitchen, I can put out my hand and grab things I need.'

(**WW**) 'Keny, my wonderful housekeeper and Girl Friday, helping me in the kitchen with the flowers and everything else.

'I've been collecting blue and white ceramics forever; a lot is on top of the cupboards. We lived next to the Portobello Road markets in London, a fabulous place to start collecting. I bought more in our travels in Europe and Asia. Both Brett and I loved the combination of blue and white; it's classic, timeless.'

The Whiteley House
at Lavender Bay

'One day, I was so fed up with Brett's painting things and spilled paint invading the entire flat, that I cleaned it all up then drew a chalk line on the floor and announced, "None of your stuff is crossing this line!" Of course, it did.'

(*WW*)

The Whiteley House at Lavender Bay

The art goddess/muse/model of the Brett and Wendy days long ago became a cultural *tour de force* in her own right, with constant demands made upon her. Wendy is generous with her time, but she can also rapidly switch to her scary *haute froideur* mood when displeased, or if she senses that someone is trying to push her around.

Wendy rarely sits still for long. Even when we've planned a long conversation, it's always interrupted by her darting up to get something, check on something with the gardeners, or deal with constant phone calls.

She likes to cook and doesn't like wasting anything, and this day when I arrive, she announces she's spent the entire previous evening making cumquat jam.

'Many citrus trees in the garden are in bloom: limes, grapefruit, blood orange trees,' Wendy begins, 'and then a huge wind blew up over the last few days and knocked half the flowers off the citrus trees, and blew away loads of the datura flowers too. I got so fed up with the wind, I harvested all the cumquats left on the trees, and made cumquat marmalade.

'I cannot believe how much time it took, how tedious it was cutting up and de-pipping the fruit, and how much sugar I used. I've made cumquat marmalade once before, and thought the sugar quantity must be wrong, so added less, and the marmalade was rather runny. This time I followed Stephanie Alexander's recipe for her mother's cumquat marmalade exactly, and it worked. It's very sticky and very sweet too, and I made a frightful mess all over the stove and kitchen, pouring it into jars. But ultimately it's very satisfying,' she pauses, 'I suppose.' She cocks her head a little with that perky Wendy smile, her blue eyes sparkling.

The sitting room at the front of the Whiteley Lavender Bay house must be one of the most famous rooms in the country. I always feel like I'm stepping into a history-soaked icon every time I enter this room.

It's not a large room. The tall windows and balcony looking out through the trees to Sydney Harbour, along with the room's ambience of elegant, languid sensuality, are still much the same as depicted in Brett Whiteley's renowned Lavender Bay paintings of the seventies and eighties. The value of these artworks has since soared to the multi-million dollar price zone.

'Brett used the smaller original sitting room as his studio when we first moved in here, all squeezed into the one-floor flat,' Wendy relates. 'It was basically the left side of the enlarged sitting room you see today. When we knocked that first interior wall down, Brett spread out further. One day, I was so fed up with Brett's painting things and spilled paint invading the entire flat that I cleaned it all up then drew a chalk line on the floor and announced, "None of your stuff is crossing this line!" Of course, it did.

'When we bought the house, Brett began to use the bottom level as his studio, but it was still too small for his big paintings, so we rented an additional large studio space nearby in the old Waverton gasworks. Then later on we bought the studio in Surry Hills.

LEFT Brett working on a charcoal drawing in the Lavender Bay house.

(**WW**) 'Brett was always very physical when he painted – he'd dance around the canvas.

'Those pants Brett is wearing might look like pyjamas, but they were actually part of a suit, in fine black velvet with white flowers. He liked wearing loose clothes, and I used to choose or make a lot of his clothes, as well as mine.

RIGHT (**WW**) 'I'm rolling on the floor in the Lavender Bay sitting room, in front of Brett's *Blue Naked Studio* (1981). I'm fooling around, having some fun with the blue naked model in the painting.

'Brett usually based his nudes on me. His earlier nudes are odalisque-like, closely related to the works of Matisse.

'People often come up to me and remark, "I've got your bum on my wall". I reply, "Seen one bum, you've seen them all!"

'This painting is huge, it took up the entire wall in our sitting room. It's now owned by David Walsh, and hanging in MONA, his museum in Tasmania.'

'Brett always loved the front sitting room, and kept using it in his paintings. In most of Brett's work, you're conscious of where the artist is. So in many interiors you'll see Brett's hand, or his hand holding a brush – he's showing you that he's inside the house or looking out to the view.'

Brett's famous wicker armchair, which in the early years graced the front sitting room when it was Brett's studio, is no longer there. (In late 2013, Brett Whiteley's Matisse-inspired painting, *My Armchair,* sold at auction in Melbourne for a record price of $3.2 million, plus the buyer's premium of $800 000.)

Wendy elaborates, 'The wicker armchair came from St Vinnie's, and Brett took it with him as his studio chair when he shifted studios. It's now in the Surry Hills Studio. Brett was fond of the notion of the artist's chair; it was like a brush that takes on its own shape as it wears in. The old wicker chair softened over time and moved with his body as he moved, rather like calligraphy.'

The interior ambiences that Brett painted were all created by Wendy. 'I always looked after the interiors of all our homes. Brett liked and admired the way I created interiors, including the "tablescapes", so he was very happy that I was always around to do this,' Wendy says. 'I've spent most of my life honing my visual intelligence, so I do know how to arrange a tabletop or a corner in a house; how to hang artworks in a house, or an exhibition in a gallery; or how to arrange a garden. Brett and I shared this strong visual intelligence, and we both understood the concept of positive and negative space.

'Brett was very game the way he left big planes of colour in many of his pictures, then had an intensity of things happening around the edges. It's not a big empty space, it's full of feeling and completely relevant to the things going on around the edges. It's a different way of seeing, a different energy from covering the entire surface with a lot of lines in the same rhythm.

'The same applies to gardens. I don't want a busy jungle, with everything shoved in together. It's important to have tranquil areas, where you sit in the middle with a shaft of sunlight, looking at all sorts of intricate things happening around the edges.'

Wendy's reasons for loving her now much-enlarged front sitting room remain the same. 'It's open, it's white, I can put good things in it, and it has great natural light,' she says.

'The light changes on Lavender Bay and the harbour quite radically. It can be dazzling sunshine with bright blue water and skies. On a rainy day the colour is more muted and grey; it's a quiet Lavender Bay day rather than a big in-your-face harbour day. If we get a clear sunset, it throws a warm orange glow over everything.'

Wendy explains that she's now knocked down so many interior walls on this level that the exposed floorboards were running in all different directions.

'So, in my last major renovation I had the floorboards overlaid with recycled wide boards all running in the same direction, then painted white and waxed. I'm very happy with it now.'

'He'd paint what was going on around him, so often it was the room as I'd arranged it, with me as the model – in the bath, on a sofa, or wherever. Not that I was lying around naked on one hip all the time!'

(*WW*)

The Whiteley House at Lavender Bay

Brett Whiteley
My Armchair, 1976
Oil on canvas, 206.5 cm x 283.5 cm
Photo: Menzies Group Auctioneers
© Wendy Whiteley

(**WW**) 'One of the earlier paintings Brett did at the Lavender Bay house. Brett's wicker armchair and that main sculpture are both now in the Brett Whiteley Studio at Surry Hills.

'The raphis palm on the right of the painting is a saga on its own. It was fiendishly expensive to buy, but too tall to fit in the room. While I was outside, Brett enterprisingly cut a hole through the floor and ceiling below, so the pot hung through the floor, suspended on its rim. We needed a garbage bin on the floor underneath, to catch the overflow when we watered it. It actually worked – lord knows how the whole thing didn't collapse.

'Sadly we also had a cat, Violet, who loved peeing on the raphis palm, and Violet killed it.'

'The wicker armchair came from St Vinnie's, and Brett took it with him as his studio chair when he shifted studios.'

(**WW**)

*The Whiteley House
at Lavender Bay*

(**WW**) 'When I look out over this balcony now, so many thoughts flood my mind. We stripped this rundown house back to its bones. It's been an amazing transformation, another alchemy.

'The original balcony was a small rotting space we enclosed with chicken wire and turned into a bird cage.

'The space to the left, with three windows, was a separate room, and Brett's original studio in this house.

'We all lived on this one floor, Brett, Arkie and me, squashed in with Brett's studio. Brett liked having us around; he was always stopping work for a chat, wandering out to see what we were doing. Brett was never the type of artist who wanted to work in total solitude.'

'I spotted the lion, half-buried in muddy water, in a deep ditch on the side of the road. It took eight Balinese men to get it out of the ditch, then it was fumigated three times and packed off to Australia to shock the Customs chaps here.'

(WW)

The Whiteley House at Lavender Bay

I've heard Wendy's style called 'haute bohemian', but to me it's just Wendy Whiteley style; she has her own aesthetic. Elegant, uncluttered and eye-catchingly different from anyone else's, with its visual seduction and harmony. She happily mixes ultramodern with antique, and ethnic artefacts with contemporary art. There's a sophistication to everything she touches, and it's all kept in impeccable order.

Brett Whiteley paintings hang on all walls in the sitting room, just as his artworks from all the stages of his career hang throughout the house. Wendy usually changes the selection of Brett's paintings in the sitting room every four months, at the same time as the exhibition changes in the Brett Whiteley Studio in inner-city Surry Hills.

'A lot of my collection of Brett's work is stored at the studio, and various works go up and down for exhibitions or are swapped from here. I like to keep the works moving around so I'm looking at different paintings. It doesn't matter how good a painting is, it can end up becoming part of the decoration if you get too used to seeing it there, and I'd never want that.'

Ruben swaps from his gardening role, using his skills as a former house painter to help with rehanging pictures in the house, filling holes and touching up walls as needed.

A conversation-stopper amidst Wendy's eclectic collection of *objets d'art* is always the life-sized, handsome old carved wooden lion she rescued from a ditch in Bali decades ago.

'I spotted the lion, half-buried in muddy water, in a deep ditch on the side of the road,' Wendy recalls. 'It took eight Balinese men to get it out of the ditch, then it was fumigated three times and packed off to Australia to shock the Customs chaps here, who fumigated it again. I think it's a Chinese temple lion that was either taken to Bali to be copied, or was carved in Bali to be a guardian in front of a temple. The lion has a very luxuriant mane and a benign presence. Kids who visit like to stroke him. I've had him mounted on a platform with wheels underneath now, so it's easy to move around wherever I want.'

Spread over the back of the comfortable lounge, beside the lion, you might find a hand-printed African mud cloth in a geometrical design of black, white and russet brown that Wendy picked up at a gallery recently, admiring the traditional skill of Mali women, who dye patterns on cloth using fermented mud. Or you might see a piece of antique batik she's had forever and has just decided to bring out.

The plush sofas and chairs in the rest of the room have large, plump cushions, and there's just the right number of fascinating things, beautifully placed, to gaze upon. Curved mirrors, mounted on either side of the main large window, will have some object like a tribal mask or a Thai bronze Buddha on a stand in front of them, with the resulting distorted reflection enhancing the viewing experience.

Native art masks from Africa, Asia and Papua New Guinea mingle on shelves beside an early gas mask. Piles of books and art magazines lie on coffee tables, waiting to be browsed.

Always, there are vases of fresh flowers and leaves. Wendy loves the purity of *Magnolia grandiflora* flowers and gathers a few whenever the large, creamy-white fragrant blooms are

low enough to pick from the big trees. Potted white *Phalaenopsis* orchids, flowering like flights of white moths, are in the sitting room year round.

A spiral staircase from the kitchen level leads up to the main bedroom. Predictably, it's no ordinary spiral staircase, but made of galvanised iron, with silvery chicken wire stretched over the sides. There's always a sense of anticipation, wondering what amazing ensemble Wendy will be wearing this time as she descends, especially when she's going to a function. Wendy doesn't just get dressed, but rather curates her entire body. It's not just the clothes, but the way she styles, ties or drapes items of clothing, selects unusual jewellery, and wraps her head in a different scarf, artistically knotted and pinned.

The bedroom is an Aladdin's Cave of Wendy's tastes. Tables are covered in rows of unusual large, chunky jewellery; necklaces, bracelets and beads. Hats and headscarves pile up like archaeological dig sites. A quaint old metal pantry cabinet, full of tiny drawers and standing on a pivot, is used to store small personal items, each drawer labelled so she knows what's inside.

There's a glamorous bathtub, of course, and it's well used. Plus a fabulous shower with a dinner-plate sized shower head. 'I need it when I come in from working in the garden, because I'm absolutely filthy,' she explains.

Most of Wendy's highly original clothes are kept in a room two levels down, on purpose-built sliding racks. Her wardrobe is nearly all black, white and blue. Clothes are organised into casual, formal, summer, winter, and outfits now relegated to gardening gear.

Above the clothes racks sit neat rows of dozens of slide-out plastic shoe boxes, each with Wendy's hand-drawn illustrated label of the shoes inside – Red Satin, Cream Suede Lace-ups, Felt Tibetan Boots, Black Kid Heels.

Wendy's office, the guestroom, guest bathroom and laundry are also on this level.

The entire house is perpetually kept in pristine order. Wendy is renowned as an obsessive housekeeper, and the ever-devoted Keny busily goes about her duties, moving from one house level to the next to keep it all just as Wendy likes it. Every couple of months, Keny's husband, Ruben, helps her to lift down all the precious blue and white ceramics from atop the high kitchen cupboards, to be dusted or washed and polished till they gleam.

Keny has been working for Wendy since 1993, and says that her daily routine is still much the same. She arrives at 7 a.m., the same time as the gardeners. 'Mostly, Wendy is already up. If not, I call out from the kitchen, "Coffee's ready," and she comes downstairs, and we eat breakfast together. We always eat breakfast and lunch together. Wendy has muesli with banana, and I have porridge. We both drink coffee, and talk about whatever is happening. Then Wendy starts reading the newspapers and dealing with her mail, messages and appointments, and I get on with the housework.'

When Keny was employed, she had no idea who Wendy was. When Ruben and others told Keny that she was working for 'the famous Wendy Whiteley', Keny's response was decidedly

'I like to keep the works moving around so I'm looking at different paintings. It doesn't matter how good a painting is, it can end up becoming part of the decoration if you get too used to seeing it there, and I'd never want that.'

(**WW**)

The Whiteley House at Lavender Bay

TOP Keny tidying up the continually occupied guest room.

BOTTOM (*WW*) 'I have an excellent study downstairs, but the view looking out onto the garden is so distracting.'

OPPOSITE (*WW*) 'I saw these carved, hand-painted North African columns and couldn't resist them. I designed my dressing room and guest bathroom around them. Most of my clothes are on slide-out racks, so they're easy to find. Likewise I've drawn illustrated labels on my shoe boxes, so I can see at a glimpse where everything is.'

228

Part of a collection of treasured personal pieces and mementos.

(**WW**) 'The vintage beaded bags were Arkie's. The intricate silver mesh bag belonged to my grandmother Julius. The bangles are Indian silver – I like wearing a lot of bracelets.'

'Everywhere Wendy puts her hands, she makes things beautiful.'

(**KENY**)

non-awestruck. She shrugs, 'I said, "Oh, ok. So?" Wendy is nice and friendly to me, very easygoing; she never puts on airs and graces. I just do my job.'

Keny admits she was somewhat baffled at first when this wealthy lady headed outside every day to work beside the gardeners, clearing up the overgrown rubbish tip in front of the house.

'I couldn't believe it at first,' Keny admits, wide-eyed. 'But then I could see that she's a different person when she can go to the garden; she's so happy, she loves it.'

For many years, all the gardeners used to join Wendy and Keny for lunch in the kitchen. But after the major renovations were finished, and the gardeners gained their own room and kitchen downstairs, they began to spend their lunch hour there.

Keny says, 'It was getting too much to have so many people for lunch every day, especially when Wendy was more and more busy with the Brett Whiteley Studio, lots of meetings and other pressures on her.'

Keny, like many people, readily admits she is hugely impressed by Wendy's artistic and design skills in the house and in the garden. 'Everywhere Wendy puts her hands, she makes things beautiful. It's so perfect. The way she arranges flowers in a vase, or puts cushions on the sofa, or moves things on the table, or arranges food on a plate.

'And her clothes, shoes and hats,' Keny rolls her eyes. 'All the racks – I say to Wendy it looks like a shop! Wendy tries on two or three outfits when she's going out somewhere special, and sometimes she calls me and asks which I think looks best. But to me she looks good in everything, especially her hats and scarves she ties around her head. Her eyes are amazing, so blue.

'She nearly always has a scarf around her hair, even at breakfast time. I'm so used to it, I've never asked her why.'

While Keny says it is fantastic to look down over the garden, she has no desire to join Wendy and the gardeners working there. 'No way please, nothing to do with me. All those ants and scratches and getting covered in dirt. I don't want to know about any problems in the garden. I am in the house.'

The main problem with the house is that Wendy's office, all the bookshelves and every storage space, is bursting at the seams with books, magazines, papers, documents and files. Wendy is trying to sort out archives, send appropriate items to the Brett Whiteley Studio, and shred others.

Much of Wendy's time in her office is spent overseeing the Brett Whiteley Estate. This requires her constant involvement with the Brett Whiteley Studio, which is managed by the Art Gallery of New South Wales, and is open free to the public three days a week, and to student and special interest groups by arrangement.

'The studio is a chance for people to go into a more intimate space, and understand the process of being a painter,' says Wendy. 'I feel an incredibly strong sense of responsibility to look after Brett's legacy: the studio, the art, this house and the garden. It's all interlinked.

The Whiteley House
at Lavender Bay

Indigenous artefacts and decorations made from seed pods, shells and woven grasses hang above the bed in the main bedroom.

(**WW**) 'In Vanuatu I bought some wonderful seed pod anklets that men use for ceremonial dancing.'

Setting up the studio was part of the concept of sharing; so was making the Secret Garden.

'I don't see any of all this as mine; I see it as something I have a responsibility for, to look after and share. I want to ensure that Brett's artworks are shared with the public, so I'm leaving my collection to the studio,' says Wendy. 'I'd be horrified if, when I'm dead, the government decided that Brett had gone out of fashion, and they sold off the collection to buy some new, fleetingly fashionable work.

'Likewise, I want the public to be able to share the Secret Garden forever more. I couldn't bear it if the government sold it off to some developer, as a prized site to build office towers or another casino.'

'I feel an incredibly strong sense of responsibility to look after Brett's legacy: the studio, the art, this house and the garden. It's all interlinked. Setting up the studio was part of the concept of sharing; so was making the Secret Garden.'

(**WW**)

The Whiteley House at Lavender Bay

LEFT (**WW**) 'The pregnant belly shapes hanging on the wall are from Mali – they're symbols of fertility.'

ABOVE (**WW**) 'I've always been into head decoration, buying antique embroidered caps from Turkey, India, Indonesia. I was a hat freak. I especially loved wearing cloche hats.

'Then Brett got into wearing hats. Sometimes he would steal my cloche hats and cut the brims off to wear them with his own brooches.

BELOW LEFT (**WW**) 'The old metal pantry cabinet has numerous small drawers, handy for storing small items.'

BELOW RIGHT (**WW**) 'I wear scarves as headwraps more often now, to keep my unruly hair off my face, and stop hair being caught in branches in the garden. I learnt a lot about headwraps from Indian men; also the Tuareg nomads of the Sahara, who wrap metres of long blue scarves around their heads in intriguing ways.'

(**WW**) 'This main bedroom, which has been through many incarnations, is now a more spacious, light-filled private retreat.

'Initially it was a small space inside the attic. We cut a hole in the floor to access the attic, then propped a fire escape ladder against the hole, so Brett and I would climb up the ladder from the floor below to go to bed.'

CHAPTER 9

Vignettes, Visitors and Volunteers

Brett Whiteley
Study for (young) wren bathing, 1988
Pen, brush and ink and wash on paper, 31.7 cm x 29.5 cm
Brett Whiteley Studio Collection
Photo: AGNSW © Wendy Whiteley

People are drawn to the Secret Garden for their own personal reasons, like Vijaya Thangaraj, known as 'the lovely Ganesh lady'.

Vijaya put a Ganesh in the garden, and daily places fresh flower offerings on the statue, sometimes ccompanied by her grand daughters, Lily and Willow.

VIJAYA THANGARAJ

Around 6.30 a.m. 'the lovely Ganesh lady', as she is known, arrives at the top of the Secret Garden with a few flowers in her hand, to perform her ritual daily ceremony.

Sometimes Vijaya Thangaraj wears a colourful Indian sari; other days it's her mammographer's uniform from the BreastScreen centre where she works.

As early morning joggers, walkers with dogs on leads and mums pushing strollers all pass by, Vijaya steps to a quiet alcove, where she starts her day by greeting the benevolent Hindu god, Lord Ganesh. She pours water on the head of the Ganesh statue, sings a Lord Ganesh song, places her offering of fresh flowers around the statue, says a special prayer, then rings a small bell hanging from a nearby handrail. She leaves with a peaceful smile on her face.

Vijaya has been known as 'the lovely Ganesh lady' for years, and the gardeners often wave hello to her and exchange smiles as they're arriving for their 7 a.m. start. Vijaya and her radiologist husband came to Australia from India in 1971, and in 2006 moved into a home unit overlooking Wendy's garden.

'One day I was carrying some wilted flowers from the Ganesh I have in my apartment, to put in a green bin, when I saw Wendy working in the garden and stopped to chat,' says Vijaya.

'Wendy explained she'd been in India and Fiji and knew all about Lord Ganesh and making offerings, and I said to her, "Next week is Lord Ganesh's birthday."'

'Wendy said, "Well, you must put a Ganesh here in the Secret Garden." So I bought a stone Ganesh statue, and Ruben fixed it permanently in place.

'Ganesh is the easiest god in Hindu belief; he blesses everyone. He is the remover of all obstacles in our lives, and also the patron of wisdom and learning new things. He has the head of an elephant, with tusks and a long trunk, a big belly and up to ten arms.

'I say a simple prayer to the garden Ganesh, "Yesterday was a good day, so please look after everyone today. Help us all have a good day, free of troublesome obstacles."

'He's not my Lord Ganesh, he's here for everyone, and so everyone can say their own small prayer and make an offering if they wish. My five grandchildren love playing in the Secret Garden, running up and down the paths, and they make offerings to Ganesh too.'

The Ganesh is so popular that numerous visitors to the garden who come across him in his secluded alcove leave more flowers, and can be heard singing, chanting and ringing his bell.

Vijaya explains another reason why the Secret Garden has such special meaning to her. 'Whenever I come here, I feel Wendy's energy is flowing to everyone, telling us that this is a garden made with great love. It is also a calm place to clear your mind amidst nature.

'If I have any problems and mixed feelings about anything, I come to the garden and when I leave I usually get a clear answer.

'I asked Wendy, "Do you meditate?" and she replied, "When I'm in the garden that's my meditation, because it's easier to work with my hands and knees in the earth and empty my mind." I understand this; as I always say, whatever problems you have, go to nature, spend some time there, and you will find the energy to pull through the day. Nature is everyone's god.'

'I asked Wendy, "Do you meditate?" and she replied, "When I'm in the garden that's my meditation, because it's easier to work with my hands and knees in the earth and empty my mind."'

(VIJAYA)

'There's a lot of
fake stuff in this world,
but there is nothing
fake about Wendy's
Secret Garden.
People love it, because
it's so personal and
so genuine.'

(GRAEME)

GRAEME DODD

Another Secret Garden regular character is 'Graeme the bike man'.

At some point most days, former antiques dealer Graeme Dodd will arrive at the Secret Garden, leading a small group of travellers he's taking on a bike tour around Sydney's iconic landmarks and hidden gems.

With his relaxed larrikin humour, Graeme will come up to Wendy while she is working in the garden, introduce today's riders from Ireland, Canada, America, Japan, China and Sweden, then proclaim to the travellers, 'Now this is Wendy Whiteley, and she's been digging away here since 1788, creating Australia's biggest guerrilla garden …'

It always brings laughter, and questions are soon flying at Wendy from the travellers, all keen to know who's funding this amazing garden, and is its future secure? Many have read about it in their home countries, on the internet and in social media, and put the Secret Garden on their Sydney trip list of must-see places.

Graeme, an enthusiastic cyclist, set up Bike Buffs in 2010 when the antiques business was in worldwide decline. He begins his tour in The Rocks, then the group pedals off with the breeze in their faces across the Harbour Bridge, stopping for photographs and commentary as they work their way around the Harbour sights to the Secret Garden, then loop back different ways to the start.

'I've never brought anyone here who's failed to be impressed with the Secret Garden,' says Graeme, 'and these are often very experienced travellers who've seen the best the world has to offer. Usually they can't stop talking about it, and asking me to send them more photographs of Wendy, and Brett's paintings and the garden. There's a lot of fake stuff in this world, but there is nothing fake about Wendy's Secret Garden. People love it, because it's so personal and so genuine.'

A mature Swedish woman with the bike group has tears pooling in her eyes as she leaves the garden. She tells me how much she enjoyed talking to Wendy, and how she sensed Wendy's motherly love throughout the garden, 'Every time Wendy touches a plant here, she's a mother stroking her daughter's hair.'

Weeds, weeds, weeds, the blight of any garden.

(**WW**) 'I always say, don't give me praise and rewards, give me some real help. Hooray for the volunteers, who come and help with the weeding.'

THE VOLUNTEERS

Over the years, praise and awards have been showered upon Wendy for making the Secret Garden. 'I've been given medals, certificates, every kind of civic gong. All very nice, and I thank them very much. But my plea is always, "Don't give me awards, please give me some real help! Come down and pick up a wheelbarrow, or bring a bucket and start weeding."'

Strangers have turned up wanting to help, but mostly it soon peters out. Many have mainly wanted to talk to Wendy and hang off her aura, so become more of a hindrance than a help.

In 2009, a few civic-minded local residents got together and decided to set up a volunteers' group, to give some genuine gardening help.

It's a sporadic arrangement, but around once a month on Saturday morning, a random group of a dozen locals, including a retired pharmacist, lawyers, a judge, an accountant and a teacher, turn up in their gardening clothes and gloves, ready to do a few hours' work.

Corrado and Ruben direct the volunteers' tasks. It's mostly weeding, but very welcome help as the weeds are relentless.

The volunteers arrive with buns and biscuits, water and thermos flasks for their morning tea break, and at lunchtime Corrado and Ruben make pizzas or barbecue Italian sausages and the volunteers toss in for the lunch costs. Conversation is swapped, and Wendy often works with them or joins them for lunch, then the volunteers head back to their own busy lives.

Retired pharmacist Geoff Pritchard and his partner Joan Street, who works in financial services, live in a nearby apartment, and have watched the Secret Garden evolve from the start.

Joan explains, 'I'm very involved with the local monthly precinct meetings, where we discuss matters of concern and send notes off to the council. It was Geoff who suggested starting the volunteers' group. He loves gardening – I actually detest it – but I'm keen to come along as a resident and do my bit to help. I bring my gloves and trowel and set to weeding and it's very rewarding. Wendy is so generous. She only has two requests. Come and enjoy the garden, and please take your rubbish away with you. Geoff and I walk a lot, and we well remember the previous unsightly, smelly, lantana-covered massive rubbish dump.

'It's amazing how Wendy's transformed it. We never dreamed the garden would get to this size, or be so beautiful and unique. Visitors do see the garden as "art in another form" – it's the most regular comment I hear. Children call it Wendy's Fairy Garden, and it fires their imagination. It's so different from a sanitised council park.

'Once I met three kids romping up the steps, so excited because they'd met Wendy when she was planting some new trees. They'd told Wendy they lived in an apartment and had no garden, so Wendy encouraged them to each plant a tree. They were thrilled to do this.'

'Once I met three kids romping up the steps, so excited because they'd met Wendy when she was planting some new trees. They'd told Wendy they lived in an apartment and had no garden, so Wendy encouraged them to each plant a tree.'

(*JOAN*)

Vignettes, Visitors and Volunteers

The volunteers enjoy the camaraderie of a lunch break, with Ruben at the barbecue.

A frequent remark is that being in the Secret Garden evokes fundamental feelings about the quality of life, and livability in our environment. You gain a strong awareness of this, looking back at towering canyons of highrise office and apartment buildings.

'I love gardening here. It's a magical place.'

(ANNETTE)

Joan mentions changes she's seen in Wendy over the two decades. 'In the early years, Wendy looked very sad, closed-off and unapproachable. Now she looks so open, and happily talks to passers-by, so it's been a positive thing for her too.'

Annette Bowman and her husband previously lived in houses with big gardens, till 2000, when they downsized to a Lavender Bay apartment with only pots on the balcony.

'I come on a morning walk past the Secret Garden, and for years I've seen Wendy out weeding and picking up rubbish before her gardeners arrive at 7 a.m.' says Annette. 'I really miss gardening, and a few years ago I asked Corrado if I could help, and he suggested I join the volunteers, so I'm now a regular,' she explains. 'I love gardening here. It's a magical place; as soon as you walk down the steps you're in a different world. The other day, parents put on a birthday party for their young daughter. They'd tied bits of tinsel, sparkly wands and stars in bushes, and organised a fairy treasure hunt. I watched these gorgeous little kids running around with shrieks of delight, and felt truly blessed to see it.'

Annette worked in cancer research, is active in community voluntary work, and her hobby is botanical art. 'I often bring my sketch pad and sit quietly, drawing. It's a lovely thing to do here.'

One very hot summer's Saturday morning, I meet some fifteen volunteers who arrive ready for action. It's been raining for the previous fortnight, and rain plus hot weather means weeds galore have sprung up everywhere, with rapid growth spurts, as only weeds know how.

Ralph Waldo Emerson, the American philosopher and nature lover, famously said, 'What is a weed? A plant whose virtues have not yet been discovered'. This theory works in vast gardens with the luxury of spaces allocated to wild meadows with weeds en masse, but it won't work in the Secret Garden.

Wendy is urging the volunteers to 'attack the sticky weed, before those long, green stalks go to seed, which means millions more of the blighters. We've got onion grass, oxalis, wandering jew, all the usual weed suspects. You can never eradicate weeds. Birds, possums bring them back too. Weeds are part of a gardener's life.'

One of the most dedicated volunteers is Ian Curdie, a semi-retired business analyst.

'I love gardens, but my prime reason for becoming involved was that I thought if the Secret Garden wasn't cherished and looked after by the community, it could just be swallowed up by the powers that be,' says Ian. 'And there really is a sense in Lavender Bay that this could happen.'

Ian has lived in Lavender Bay for twenty-nine years, and has observed Wendy's garden evolve from the beginning. 'It's been quite amazing to watch it push further along the bay,' he says. 'The Secret Garden has its different charms, depending on the time of day that you are down there. I find it particularly beautiful just walking around the terraced paths that trace through the back slope of the valley, seeing the sun filtering through the green of the canopy

The volunteers toss in for lunch, but always request Corrado to bring the tasty sausages from his Italian butcher.

and striking bright red leaves or something else. The amazing explosions of colour and light are so attractive, and inspiring too.

'All Wendy's strange combinations in the garden are so arresting. The plants, and the way paths and staircases merge, veer out again, or zigzag up and down. Then there's the delight of the found objects she's unearthed. So many things await to be discovered.'

Ian happily weeds, or helps spread piles of mulch. 'Truth to tell, gardening isn't my first love,' he admits. 'But I enjoy gardening in the Secret Garden more because of the company of the other gardeners. You don't get that when you're just slaving around the garden in your own home. It's a good feeling to be bonding with your local community, helping care for a place we should all cherish.'

The best contact for anyone wanting to join the volunteers is lavenderbayprecinct@gmail. com. North Sydney has several local residents precinct groups, and this is the email address for the local Lavender Bay precinct group, who started this volunteer group.

THE MAP OF THE GARDEN

When I started work on this book, it was obvious that we needed a good map of the Secret Garden. None existed; not even a rudimentary sketch.

Wendy and her gardeners all agreed a map was long overdue, as there's endless confusion over which part of the garden they're discussing.

Corrado groans, 'Wendy will say, "I want you to prune the lemon tree". I'll ask, "Which lemon tree?"

'Wendy will answer, "You know, the one at the bottom of the steps". I'll say, "Which steps?"'

Corrado had just been through the roundabout trying to locate the nest of bull ants that stung one of the women volunteer gardeners.

She: 'It's near the dead tree.' He: 'There's two dead trees here now.' She: 'Near the fence.' He: 'Which fence?' She: 'The tall metal fence.' He: 'Which part of the fence?' She: 'Near the gardeners' sheds.' He: 'OK. Now I know where you mean.'

But the Secret Garden lives up to its name, in that mapping it is easier said than done.

Aerial photography gives no clues as to what lies underneath. The tree canopy is so dense, you can barely spot a path, nor get any sense of the terrain dipping into a steep-backed valley.

On the ground, the myriad of interlinking paths and staircases are like a giant game of snakes and ladders. So much is intriguingly camouflaged by trees and thick vegetation that you cannot see very far ahead where paths and steps go, as they meander up, down, across and around the winding valley.

'I love gardens, but my prime reason for becoming involved was that I thought if the Secret Garden wasn't cherished and looked after by the community, it could just be swallowed up by the powers that be.'

(*I A N*)

Local landscape architect John Chetham so admires the unorthodox way Wendy has made the Secret Garden, he took on the head-spinning task of mapping it.

(*JC*) 'This garden follows a strong international philanthropic tradition of taking a piece of blighted land and transforming it into an iconic landscape and a wonderful community facility.'

*'Wendy's garden
is singing out,
"Let's have charm,
informality, spirit and
feeling in a garden;
come in here and
enjoy being in
a different place."'*

(*JOHN*)

So the map went into the too-hard basket for long months. A keen young horticulturalist from the council made a valiant attempt at a map, but it needed additional professional expertise.

Landscape architect John Chetham came to the rescue. Five years earlier he'd moved into an office in Harbourview Crescent, on the top edge of the Secret Garden, and was elated to discover Wendy's creation.

He walks through the Secret Garden daily, stops to chat with the gardeners, and is often a friendly source of advice on a particular tree or plant species.

'I celebrate and love the way Wendy has thumbed her nose at all the formality of landscape design, ignored all the codes, broken the rules and regulations – and her garden is an absolute triumph!' John Chetham says with a huge grin.

'Wendy has created a personal, idiosyncratic garden with her own aesthetic rules and cavalier approach to petty bureaucratic regulations. Visitors respond to this, they see it's different, and utterly love it. What's more, no one's ever had an accident here – they look where they're going, and use their common sense.'

John agrees with Wendy that art organised by committees looks bland, as do gardens organised by committees.

John speaks of his frustration designing public parks and gardens today. 'The nanny state health and safety rules and regulations are so restricting about the size, height, width, depth of each step, each handrail, each path, the materials you're allowed to use. Cost-cutting often means you can only plant a border of one homogenous species, and only plant trees that don't drop leaves, flowers or seeds, or make a mess. Everything has to be minimal maintenance. It means public parks and gardens run the risk of becoming sterile places.

A local resident who walks her small, pale-haired dog lifts her panting pooch up to let it splash in the birdbath as a regular treat.

'Wendy's garden is singing out, "Let's have charm, informality, spirit and feeling in a garden; come in here and enjoy being in a different place." So people come here from far and wide, and I see the genuine happiness on their faces.'

With the help of two students in his office, John started on the garden map. It was a painstakingly slow process, squaring up the garden in small sections, then measuring all the features and then drawing it up. 'When you're inside the garden, attempting to remember where the maze of erratic staircases goes, you feel like Harry Potter trying to navigate the giant moving staircases inside Hogwarts Castle,' John says, laughing.

'Even after we thought we had the map fairly complete, when we showed it to Ruben and Corrado, they picked out a few places where we had a missing staircase or part of a twisting path in the wrong position. It makes me think of that nursery rhyme – there was a crooked man and he walked a crooked mile.'

John says, 'Wendy's Secret Garden follows a strong international philanthropic tradition of taking a piece of blighted land, and transforming it into an iconic landscape and a wonderful community facility. Wendy's made one of the best community gardens in Australia, up there with the best by world standards, and it's a magnificent act of philanthropy on her part. It's a winner on all counts.'

He hopes the Secret Garden can continue forever more, with its pristine standard of romantic perfection. 'This garden is so perfect in its juxtapositions of colour and form, and in all its subtle intricacies,' John says, 'which also means it requires high maintenance by a dedicated team of gardeners, who work with passion.

'When Wendy has departed this earth, and is bossing the gardening team about from up in the heavens, the Secret Garden will always need someone in charge who understands the chemistry between Wendy's artistry, the hard work, and the passion.'

Meanwhile, people continue each day to form their own private relationships with their special nooks in the garden. Each morning as Vijaya puts fresh flowers on Lord Ganesh, a lawyer who lives in a nearby apartment unrolls his yoga mat on a calm, grassy patch to start his meditation routine, and a small group begin Tai Chi exercises.

Vijaya says Lord Ganesh has become so popular, his alcove is sometimes carpeted in flowers.

'Someone is coming during the day and putting a red kumkum dot on his forehead. I am happy about this, as the red dot on a god's forehead symbolises opening the third eye to beauty.'

A young woman, heading off to Paris to live indefinitely, held a farewell picnic for her closest friends, to give away all the clothes she wasn't taking with her.

Artists from the Royal Art Society, which has an office, art school and gallery nearby, arrive with drawing and painting materials. They ponder various vistas, then settle down to work *en plein air* on images of the garden and the harbour.

A young couple return to the Secret Garden every year on their wedding anniversary, to sit together and paint a scene of this garden of love.

'When you're inside the garden, attempting to remember where the maze of erratic staircases goes, you feel like Harry Potter trying to navigate the giant moving staircases inside Hogwarts Castle.'

(*JOHN*)

Vignettes, Visitors and Volunteers

ROMANCE

Always, there are signs of romance in the garden. It's become a popular spot to propose, and in rather more inventive ways than on bended knee.

One Sunday morning, I spot this tableau in a nook near the big stand of bamboo. A single red rose has been placed on the table, and beside it a red gift bag with a red balloon floating above.

A young man sitting on a bench nearby explains that he is guarding his friend's elaborate eight-stage marriage proposal. The suitor has taken his girlfriend to breakfast at the Opera House, they're coming over the bridge to walk through Wendy's Secret Garden, where he will woo her with the red rose and gift. Inside are two tickets to ride the Ferris Wheel in nearby Luna Park. Then it's on to a boat for lunch, then to sail away to a beachside dinner, where he will finally propose. 'She'd better say yes!' the friend concludes.

He adds that he knows Wendy's Secret Garden well, and comes here regularly to think through university assignments for his special education course.

A few weeks later, this book's photographer Jason Busch comes across another romantic proposal tableau. A white rug is lying on the grass, with cushions, a white table, a vase of white roses, ice bucket of champagne, two glasses and strawberries. It obviously worked.

A large card has been left propped against the table, announcing, 'She said yes'.

Weddings, weddings and more weddings are happening in the Secret Garden, so much so that permission is now required from North Sydney Council, to keep a check on the number. Many weddings decorate a part of the garden for the ceremony, tying ribbons and extra bunches of flowers onto trees and bushes. They organise string quartets, cellists, harpists and singers. Others hand out white parasols or glamorous hats for every guest, and bring in chairs for the ceremony.

Often there's a bunch of wedding flowers and a note left tied to Wendy's house gate, thanking her for making the garden. It is a place that allows treasured memories to be created in so many other people's lives.

16/4.73
BW

CHAPTER 10

Wendy's Gift

Brett Whiteley
Beach Study, 1973
Ink on paper, 43.5 cm x 27.5 cm
Private collection
Photo: Val Foreman
© Wendy Whiteley

Sometimes the story of a garden is also the story of a life, and so it is with Wendy Whiteley's Secret Garden.

The tiny secret garden that seven-year-old Wendy burrowed inside a bamboo thicket in her backyard to nurture her childhood imagination has now come full circle, and evolved into the huge Lavender Bay Secret Garden she's been creating since 1992.

Wendy's Secret Garden carries an inspiring metaphor, as it's brought about a double regeneration. It's seen the regeneration of Wendy Whiteley from a grief-ravaged shell into a calmer, fuller person with a kinder wisdom and a more encompassing sense of happiness and fulfilment. And it has delivered the magical regeneration of a once-ravaged site in Lavender Bay, transforming it into a unique tranquil haven that members of the public now cherish.

'Good on you, State Railways, for keeping this land vacant for so long, giving me the chance to fix it up,' Wendy says, her face spreading into a smile as she stands in front of her huge guerrilla garden. 'And good on you State Railways again, if you very kindly hand over to North Sydney Council this vacant land that you've never used since 1890, so it can become a permanent public park.'

Wendy Whiteley's Secret Garden at Lavender Bay is now a well-established, sought-out Sydney landmark with an international reputation.

While the Secret Garden is absolutely Wendy Whiteley's oeuvre, Brett Whiteley's spirit is also forever there: in every glistening Moreton Bay fig leaf, languid palm tree, fragrant frangipani and seductive harbour glimpse.

'Brett's here, and Arkie's here with me in the garden,' Wendy says lovingly. 'I have happy thoughts about them both and feel very close to them. They both stay forever young and beautiful in my mind, whilst I grow older and older and my limbs begin to creak.'

Brett was entranced by the ultramarine vision and tranquillity of Lavender Bay, the curvilinear harmony of the water's edge, the Bridge and Opera House, the boats with their trails of wash and circling birdlife.

In one of his artist's notebooks, Brett wrote, 'Two-thirds of Braque's work is tabletops, there's Morandi's bottles, Lloyd Rees's hills … My repeating theme – a subject I will always go back to until I die – Lavender Bay.'

Brett's lyrical paintings of Sydney Harbour and Lavender Bay have become classic national icons, representing Australia's beloved harbour and sensual, summery identity.

The linkage of Brett and Wendy Whiteley's creative oeuvres – Brett's paintings and Wendy's Secret Garden – now offers a vast, glorious Whiteley artwork for public enjoyment. This Lavender Bay ensemble of both Brett and Wendy's work into one huge Australian cultural icon seems as though it was destined to be.

Wendy reflects, 'I doubt I could have made this garden if Brett was still alive and we'd stayed together. We were both so busy living life, and Brett's art and everything associated with it took up most of our time. I believed in his art so strongly that it truly did absorb most of both our lives.'

> 'Good on you,
> State Railways,
> for keeping this land
> vacant for so long,
> giving me the chance
> to fix it up.'
> (WW)

Wendy's Gift

This young woman was moving to Paris, and, in the buoyant spirit of her new adventure, held a party in the Secret Garden to give away her clothes.

A myriad of different personal reasons draws visitors to the Secret Garden. Wendy observes, 'I see it in many people – that they are responding to something other than the actual garden – they're responding more to something inside themselves that the garden evokes.

'Perhaps it's knowing that it began as a garden associated with private grieving. But it's not an elegiac garden; it's gone far beyond this and grown into a life-affirming gift garden for everyone to share.

'And it's a garden made by one woman; not by a committee or a council, or a professional landscape designer for a client. It's made by one obsessive woman, approaching it like a painting. But you can't control a garden the way you can control a painting; the garden is alive and always changing itself with a force of its own. And you can't control the weather, which might sabotage your vision or help it along.'

Often, I hear people express how they love being alone in a garden, listening to their own drifting thoughts. One strong appeal of Wendy's garden lies in the way it allows this, by offering private recesses like tiny leafy chapels. Places to tuck yourself away, enjoy the calm solitude and rebalance your day, places to reflect on simple truths or contemplate profound thoughts. Perhaps to experience one of those small epiphanies that bring meaning to our lives.

'I see it in many people – that they are responding to something other than the actual garden – they're responding more to something inside themselves that the garden evokes.'

(WW)

'I constantly see people walking into the garden, looking stressed and wary about the state of the world or their own lives,' says Wendy. 'Then they glimpse something joyous, like new buds bursting on a branch, or a wattle bird probing its slim curved bill inside flowers to sip nectar. Then they decide, well, the world isn't such a terrible place after all.

'So the garden is communicating something other than itself. That's what art is all about, a work of art communicates something other than itself. A painting isn't finished until it's viewed; a book isn't finished until it's read; a garden isn't finished until it's shared.

'I hope that people who come here find it inspiring, and leave wanting to do something more in their own lives. I know that creating this garden has changed me, and I'm very grateful.'

I've heard many international travellers compare Wendy's Secret Garden with the High Line in New York. Both are immensely successful urban renewal projects dreamed up and forged by inspired amateurs; and therein lies their special appeal. Interestingly, both sites have their genesis in railways.

The High Line is a 2.5 kilometre-long elevated public park, created on a disused freight rail line in Manhattan's Lower West Side. It was due to be demolished, when artist Robert Hammond and travel writer Joshua David, who lived in the neighbourhood, had a crazy dream that it could be saved and revitalised as a public park.

The pair had no experience in urban planning or landscape architecture, but their immense enthusiasm turned the crazy dream into a reality. Hammond maintains that having no professional skills was an advantage. The charm of the High Line comes from the fact that it

Wendy's Gift

258

was started from the bottom up, by amateurs. Later on, New York City became involved. But he says if city authorities had started the project from the top down, the High Line would never have been as innovative and personalised as it now is.

Wendy echoes Hammond's notion: that if government authorities had converted the Lavender Bay wasteland into a park, it would have been another sanitised, over-regulated public park, instead of her wonderfully crazy artistic dream.

Wendy's dilemma today is that the Secret Garden has become so well-known; copious numbers of spellbound Australian and international visitors have posted photographs and comments on internet websites and blogs. So it's become difficult for Wendy to work in the garden undisturbed and incognito, the way she prefers, in old clothes and with a scarf tied around her head.

When visitors spot Wendy working alone or beside her gardeners and feel the urge to say something, most are charming, respectful, even humble in the way they approach her. I've seen numerous people with glowing faces go up to her and simply say, 'Thank you Wendy, thank you for making the garden. It's beautiful.'

Wendy periodically tries to stop and chat, but admits, 'It's getting harder now with so many people wanting to talk to me. If I stop and talk to them all I'll never get any work done. Most ask the same questions, expecting me to go over the history of the garden again and again. I'll be delighted to be able to say – please just go and read the book!

'I do have a great empathy with the gardening groups who visit. But when they expect me to rattle out botanical names for plants, I'm useless, as I've forgotten them or never bothered learning them in the first place. I don't mean to sound ungrateful, because through this garden I've met all sorts of people I'd never normally have met, especially people from outside the art world.'

Frequently someone will appear from Wendy's past, using the garden as a way to reconnect with her. 'Someone will come up saying, "Do you remember me, we were at primary school together?"

'Others make a real effort to find me, because they want to tell me something about Brett, or Arkie. Women in particular have told me they've endured some terrible tragedy, then found that starting a garden can bring crucial nourishment and purpose into their lives to help them carry on. I'm touched by their stories, and would love to invite them up to the house for a cup of tea and a long chat, but these days I just don't have time.'

Wendy admits her pleasure when certain people have reconnected with her via the garden. 'One day I was dead-heading roses, snip, snip, snip with the secateurs, when Robert Graves' son, Juan, turned up to say hello. It's over thirty years since I last saw him, as a teenager in Majorca. We soon reminisced about evenings spent together in Deia, when Brett and I went to Majorca in the summers and always visited the wonderful old poet Robert Graves and his family.'

'I do have a great empathy with the gardening groups who visit. But when they expect me to rattle out botanical names for plants, I'm useless, as I've forgotten them or never bothered learning them in the first place.'
(WW)

Within the Secret Garden you can find contentment, peace of mind, reflective thoughts, rapture.

(*WW*) 'You can engage in the art of looking. So many people look, but they don't see. It was the only thing I learnt at school that made immediate sense.'

Occasionally there are bad days which leave Wendy and the gardeners heartbroken, when vandals deliberately trample the garden or smash furniture and handrails.

'On those days I wish I could fence the garden off, and say, "You're not allowed in here because you don't behave properly,"' says Wendy. '"This garden is a gift to enjoy. We only ask, please clean up your own mess and your dogs' mess, and don't go off your head drinking and taking drugs and becoming destructive."'

If Wendy spots partying teenagers coming into the garden, clearly off their heads on something, she's been known to deliver them a fearsome lecture. 'One night, Anna Schwartz and Professor Marcia Langton were here, and the three of us went down and told off a group of drunken kids for being so stupid. They must have thought we were the three Witches of Eastwick,' Wendy chortles. 'They looked terrified of us, and skedaddled.'

The vast majority of visitors to the Secret Garden still assume the council or the government is paying for the gardeners, plants and everything, and have no idea that Wendy has funded the entire project from day one, and continues to do so. She's now poured millions of dollars into it, plus her own invaluable labour.

The odd visitor treats Wendy's gardeners as if they are public staff, on duty to be ordered about. I witnessed this one day when I'd joined the gardeners during their lunch break, in their retreat inside the gardeners' room in the basement level of Wendy's house. From here the gardeners can look back through the house gate to the Secret Garden, and keep an eye on things.

This lunch break was loudly interrupted by two ladies calling out from the house gate, in imperious voices. Corrado put down his hot pasta lunch and courteously went over to them.

The ladies announced they were from a garden group, and required a full tour of the garden on a certain date next month that suited their members. For over five minutes they outlined wet weather options and other arrangements, addressing Corrado in a below-the-stairs manner, as if this was an episode from *Downton Abbey.*

Corrado was unfailingly polite as his lunch went cold, and said he'd provide a tour of the garden. This means interrupting his own work, but good-hearted Corrado is always willing to show genuinely interested people around.

The two ladies conferred as they started to leave, then one called back, upping her imperious tone whilst stressing, 'We require *Wendy* to lead our tour. We have important members in our group, so *it must be Wendy* who leads us around.'

'Yes luv,' Corrado responded, all Italian charm with an obliging wave. 'I'll tell Wendy, I'll tell the boss.' The lady looked quite taken aback by the gardener calling her 'luv', and I tried to contain a moment of mirth as I watched the expression on her face.

The basement level of Wendy's house is now also crammed with large storage crates of letters, photographs and mementos that visitors have sent Wendy or left at her gate. These continue to grow, as do the messages and drawings left in the Secret Garden visitors' books. Some deeply

'One night, Anna Schwartz and Professor Marcia Langton were here, and the three of us went down and told off a group of drunken kids for being so stupid. They must have thought we were the three Witches of Eastwick.'

(WW)

personal letters from older writers mention that visiting Wendy's Secret Garden has evoked their own childhood memories of reading *The Secret Garden* by Frances Hodgson Burnett.

Wendy is touched by these letters and messages and says, 'This is a garden full of love and emotion. Everyone who comes here feels it, and so does everyone who works here with me. None of us were professional gardeners. We've all learned from nature, the plants and the birds, bugs and bees as we made the garden. Just like that bossy little girl in *The Secret Garden*.'

Laughing at herself she adds, 'And I've reinvented myself as a bag lady gardener, down here daily in old clothes with a bit of rag tied round my head, and living above my workplace in a very comfortable shed.'

A momentous milestone occurred in March 2014. Wendy stopped smoking! Hooray! Finally, at seventy-two, she quit her lifetime habit of two-plus packs a day. She quit cold turkey; no patches and no aids. 'I do everything to extremes,' Wendy remarks, shrugging it off with her sparkle-eyed grin. For long years, Wendy's friends and the gardeners have worried about Wendy's continuous smoking and often hacking cough. 'She gave up heroin, but she can't quit cigarettes,' was repeated countless times.

My attempts to raise the topic with Wendy were always smartly batted back. 'Yes, I smoke like a chimney, it's the only vice left for an ageing woman … don't *tell* me to stop, I'm no good when people *tell* me to do things.'

Wendy's sudden quitting occurred when she had to go into hospital for surgery that required a full anaesthetic, and she was forbidden to smoke during her hospital stay.

'I saw a lung specialist before I left hospital, and I said to him, "I suppose you're going to tell me to quit smoking permanently?"' Wendy relates.

'He was very clever with me. He didn't *tell* me, "You must stop or you'll be dead". He only said, "Look, of course you should stop, but I know what you're like, so just do whatever you can". So I thought, hmmph, bugger you, I'll show you – I'll stop. And I did.'

Having quit nicotine, Wendy decided she'd also quit dyeing her hair auburn, and go grey gracefully. So for the next several months, she was forever in a headscarf or hat in public, while she began growing her hair out to its natural grey.

While Keny was thrilled that Wendy had at last quit smoking, she was less thrilled with her boss's decision to go grey. 'I said to Wendy, "Do you want me to tell you the truth? It's a terrible idea! What for?"'

Keny has been dyeing Wendy's hair for several years, since the first streaks of grey invaded. 'Wendy got irritated at how many hours it took having her hair dyed in the hairdressing salon, so I said, "I'll do it for you. I'll be a hairdresser too. No worries." But Wendy's hair grows so slowly, it's going to take her a year to grow it out … so we'll see if she changes her mind!'

It's one of those glorious, shimmering midsummer days, when I'm in the garden with Wendy, watching a white-faced heron's slow, bouncing flight as it lands on a rock ledge near the bird bath.

'I've reinvented myself as a bag lady gardener, down here daily in old clothes with a bit of rag tied round my head, and living above my workplace in a very comfortable shed.'

(WW)

Wendy's Gift

(**WW**) 'The Secret Garden offers both company and solitude; time to listen to your own thoughts. It allows you to immerse yourself in all the scents and sensations of nature; savour the subtle pleasures.

'It fulfils the desire we all have to feel secluded, enclosed, and sheltered from the turbulent events of the world outside. Even if it's only for a brief time, we can retain the peace of the experience.'

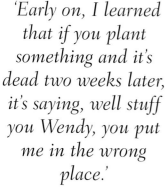

(**WW**) 'When I started on the Secret Garden, the only birds I ever saw were small blue wrens under the lantana thickets, seagulls and pigeons. As the garden flourished and grew larger, so did the varieties of birds flocking in. Rainbow lorikeets were early arrivals.'

'Early on, I learned that if you plant something and it's dead two weeks later, it's saying, well stuff you Wendy, you put me in the wrong place.'

(**WW**)

This prompts a rollcall of the local wildlife now frequenting the Secret Garden.

'I've never seen a snake,' Wendy begins. 'Lots of rats. In the early years we'd see big harbour rats in the old sandstone harbour drain pit. Now we only see bush rats. Lots of lizards, lazy old blue tongues. Lots of birds. We used to have Indian mynas, then mobs of Australian noisy miners drove away the Indian mynas, pecking and scolding them. Rainbow lorikeets flock in when the palms and coral trees are flowering. We have laughing kookaburras, hooting owls, buff-banded rail birds scampering into the undergrowth. Some years a lot of currawongs, other years lots of magpies. They're all competing for real estate and in the end they all have a good squabble and sort it out. A pair of king parrots has been reappearing for years and years, and now we have brush turkeys too.

'We have possums, ringtail and brushtail. We've all been bitten by big bull ants and little spiders, but never seen a funnel-web spider, thank goodness.

'We get termites chomping the old railway sleepers, so we have to replace them. And more chomping old tree trunks, and my house balcony, which I had to replace in the big renovation.'

Moving along to a rollcall of plants, Wendy mentions, 'Early on, I learned that if you plant something and it's dead two weeks later, it's saying, "Well stuff you Wendy, you put me in the wrong place." So now I move things when I see they aren't happy, they need more sun, or more shade, or different soil.

'Other things I've planted have immediately gone "Voom!", with their chests puffed out, and five years on I'm clipping away at them with pruning shears, because I've planted them too close together and now they're enormous.

'We've learned what works here, and we've all learned to become better gardeners. Our bodies are still holding up, though Corrado and I both worry about our knees, and I've ruined my hands. No matter what gardening gloves I wear, I get scratched wrists and my nails are perpetually black, which is the giveaway for gardeners.'

Ambling along a path as it weaves beneath the canopy, Wendy remarks that the garden is now growing so well, many parts are Rousseau-like.

'We need to prune and let more light in, or the plants underneath will get mouldy,' she says. 'The bird's nest ferns under the canopy don't want too much sun, but if you give them a little bit of sun they double in size. Our bird's nest ferns are now mammoths, like in a rainforest.'

In early 2014, two huge coral trees had to be cut down, as borers and rot had rendered them in danger of falling. A massive cacophony of noise from chainsaws and mulcher marked the full-day operation. At the conclusion, Wendy was seen clowning for the workmen, standing on the coral tree stump like a statue on a plinth.

'Now so much sunlight is coming down in the patches where the coral trees cast shade, that we had to revise these parts so tender plants don't get sunburnt,' Wendy explains.

She's still obsessively changing things, honing, finessing; fixing up things that her unerring aesthetic eye and painterly hands decide could be better.

Early narrow goat-track paths are being widened. Some early efforts at making steps up steep sections are now sinking or sloping, so need realigning.

'I'm evening up the harmony in some staircases, so the visual appeal is more pleasing,' says Wendy. 'Mere maintenance is boring. I need to keep creating.'

The good-natured banter and occasional squabbling continues between Wendy and her loyal team of gardeners. They know that Wendy's artistry can make a simple thing, like a garden path or a staircase winding up the hillside, seem full of beauty and meaning.

Several younger gardeners have now worked alongside Ruben and Corrado, and become trained in the ways of the Secret Garden. I watch Corrado carefully folding back the petals on a rose to show Jay Jay a cluster of tiny black beetles hiding inside the flower, after these culprits have taken big bites out of each leaf on the bush.

'You've gotta spray these beetles, before they get on all the other plants and eat them too,' he instructs. Jay Jay is studying horticulture part-time, but knows he also has much to learn from his self-taught peers.

Corrado's heart still bleeds when he sees plants, especially citrus trees, becoming sickly, or dying. When he's happy, he loudly whistles entire songs, including the Italian National Anthem. Ruben reckons he always knows how to find Corrado in the garden by his whistles, or by the ringtone on his mobile phone – it plays the Italian National Anthem.

As for a rollcall on herself, Wendy sighs, then reflects, 'I feel much more peaceful in myself these days. When I was younger, I used to be very quick-tempered. I was always averse to the middle ground in anything. I had strong intellectual biases and taste biases. Now I don't want that kind of baggage.

'I've become more understanding, less biased, and more mellow. The middle ground is often where I'd rather be. So now I don't overreact to things that happen, or take it too personally.

'I've invested in kindness, in a way that I thought I was too smart to do before. It takes a good kick up the arse, like being an addict for thirteen years then getting off heroin, to teach you some humility and to recognise the need to be kind to everyone else.'

So, does Wendy think she's finally found her best self?

'There's no finality to that question. You're always looking,' she responds.

'Though I'm no saint. Sometimes I get impatient, grumpy, and fed-up with being so nice answering visitors' questions, when I'd rather be uninterrupted and gardening with my own thoughts.

'I think it's been good for me to do something where I lose myself, and feel physically exhausted at the end of the day. I try not to go backwards too much emotionally, or have too many expectations for the future. I think that living in the day is a brilliant notion.

'See that today is a beautiful day, and don't waste it by sitting in a dark room feeling sorry for yourself. Don't waste time on negative energy. Get outside in the sunshine, there's a helluva lot on offer out there, all for free. Do something positive. Creating something is an act of freedom.'

'I've invested in kindness, in a way that I thought I was too smart to do before. It takes a good kick up the arse, like being an addict for thirteen years then getting off heroin, to teach you some humility and to recognise the need to be kind to everyone else.'

Wendy's Gift

PLEASE CLEAN UP AFTER
YOURSELF AND YOUR
DOG THANKYOU.

(**WW**) 'Starting a garden is a sign of hope, that it will grow and last.'

(**WW**) 'In gardens, you are involved in a relationship with the earth itself. So we've all grown: me, my gardeners, friends and visitors, along with the Secret Garden. Let yourself love a garden, and you can find enduring happiness.'

(**WW**) 'Did I have any idea what I'd started? It's quite humbling looking at that picture now of a forlorn woman standing alone on a bleak site and thinking how my life has changed, along with that piece of land.

'I suppose the message is, whatever terrible things seem to overwhelm your life, don't give in and feel sorry for yourself. Get outside into the fresh air, get a move on, and do something positive.'

People often ask Wendy, if she hadn't done the garden, what might have become of her? She replies, 'The answer is that I have no idea. I made an absolute decision not to sell the house and try to reinvent myself, because that's impossible. You are who you are because of the entire tapestry of your life – good, bad and indifferent.

'Making the garden was something useful I could do – instead of uselessly getting obsessed with house-cleaning and renovations, or sitting around staring at my navel thinking, "Poor me, I've lost my husband and my daughter, I'm a victim of life". I've never admired self-pity in anyone.

'Sometimes events like the death of your daughter seem so unfair, so unjust, that it's beyond explaining. It just is what it is. That's all you can say.'

Wendy says that she had to force herself to step back and not become too angry and judgemental about life. 'You have to think, well, that's today, and tomorrow will be different; and it usually is.

'I don't think you ever stop grieving. But look around and you'll see people who've changed their grieving process from debilitating hopelessness into something positive and beautiful.

'Some people see the garden as my therapy, but it's not only that. Or if it started off as therapy, it's gone way beyond that. It's also a very strong desire to do something new and creative to share with other people, rather than just repeat yourself and go backwards all the time. Starting a garden is a sign of hope, that it will grow and last.'

One afternoon, I'm sitting at the kitchen table with Wendy, looking through boxes of
photographs taken in the early years of clearing the garden site. We also have a computer slide
show of the wonderful photographs that Jason Busch has been taking of the Secret Garden
over the past eighteen months.

In the early photographs, there's a picture of Wendy, twenty-three years younger, in gumboots
and work clothes, standing on a woeful-looking barren slope that she's been clearing beneath
the big Moreton Bay fig tree. More pictures show the inland side of the steep valley, an almost
bare slope of landfill sandstone rubble, after Wendy, Corrado, Ruben, Chantal and Luke have
finally cleared it and carted away masses of rubbish.

It looks one vast, barren wasteland, a massively daunting task to even know where or
how to begin the fledgling garden. Where to start digging and making terraces on steep
hillsides, where to put paths and steps, where to create designs and patterns of planting,
let alone how to create an intimate atmosphere of sophisticated artistry, romance, whimsy
and a sense of magic, so children can believe that fairies might live here.

That forlorn, barren valley is almost unrecognisable, compared to the glorious verdant
foliage and trees that fill it, now transformed into the Secret Garden. The contrast between
the 'before' and 'after' photographs is truly overwhelming, to see what Wendy and her gardeners
have achieved in that time.

Ruben and Corrado come in to look at the photographs, and begin to reminisce. Wendy
gives them a fond hug, and their faces shine with pride as she says, 'It just feels so good to look
at the Secret Garden today, then think back over the past twenty-three years and be able to
say, "I'm glad we did it", rather than, "Oh, I wish we had done it."'

When Wendy stands by herself in the garden at sunset, and the last rays of golden light slant
through the trees, she feels an immense closeness to Brett and Arkie. Their ashes are scattered
in the garden, but it's more than this, she says.

'Their spirits are here in Lavender Bay and trees are growing out of their spirits.'

I ask if she thinks Brett would have been proud of her for creating this garden.

'On a good day, yes,' Wendy answers, smiling.

'Brett would have loved the Secret Garden, and all the birdlife it has attracted. He wouldn't
have raked any leaves or done any weeding, but he would have made some lovely drawings.

'Brett was fascinated with alchemy, the act of altering something from one state to another.
Alchemy is one of his iconic paintings.

'Making the Secret Garden is my piece of alchemy,' says Wendy, 'because I transformed
a ghastly old rubbish dump into a beautiful garden. And along the way, in return, the garden
transformed me.'

*'Making the Secret
Garden is my piece
of alchemy because
I transformed a ghastly
old rubbish dump into
a beautiful garden.
And along the way,
in return, the garden
transformed me.'*

(**WW**)

Some messages written in the Visitors' Books left on the table below the entry to the Secret Garden. Wendy invites all visitors to write or draw their thoughts, and says she is thrilled when visitors express real appreciation for the garden.

(**WW**) 'A garden is not just a place where flowers grow. It's a place of perception, about everything in the garden, and a lot within ourselves.

'I remember that bossy little girl in *The Secret Garden* book I read as a child had become much nicer by the end of the story. She said that if you look the right way, you can see the whole world is a garden.'

Afterword

Janet Hawley

In early 2013, when Wendy and I sat at her kitchen table discussing how I planned to write this book, Wendy stopped me and said, 'Now I want to say something personal to you. I think you should let it be known that this book has an emotional connection to you too – because I'm sure that it does.

'I've long thought that you've always shown a great amount of empathy towards women who've survived extreme circumstances, then dealt with loss in a positive way. I've seen it in the way you've written about many people over the years … including Picasso's partner Françoise Gilot, and myself.

'And you've always written about the Secret Garden *with heart,* some special connection. It's never been *just work* for you, or writing with your head. I've never known where these feelings inside you came from, but I think you should explain it in the book.'

That's Wendy, ever perceptive about people's private zones.

And it is true, so – with some reluctance – I explained it. I had a childhood secret garden of my own, a treasured retreat inside the green curtains of a huge weeping willow tree. The willow and giant tree ferns grew beside the waterfall on the creek running behind my childhood home.

My mother Margot Hawley's great love, indeed her life's work, was the glorious, rambling garden that she created on four acres of land in St Ives, in the era when St Ives was still a quiet, semi-rural backwater on Sydney's upper North Shore. The land was part of an abandoned orchard, spilling into a large valley overgrown with giant blackberry bushes, lantana and tangled morning glory vines. Behind this was a large forest, where my two brothers and I wandered and played with no sense of fear.

I was six years old when Margot started clearing the land, with the help of two cheerful Italian migrant labourers, both called Giuseppe.

They gradually freed the smothered creek and valley, untangling vines from enormous trees, then terraced the valley with its own bush rocks, and planted cascades of climbing roses, lavenders, hydrangeas, and more weeping willows along the creek. Garden beds and blossom tree walks were laid out in the old orchard. Over the next twenty-five years, creating her garden was Margot's consuming passion and a source of great happiness to her, as well as to her husband Arthur, family and friends. It all came to a sudden, tragic end when I was thirty-one; my mother's life, and her glorious garden.

Happily, the story of Wendy's Secret Garden is the reverse. What began with tragedy has grown with enthusiasm, purpose and ever-expanding public acclaim into a place that brings immense pleasure and solace to vast numbers of people.

As Wendy says, each person who visits the Secret Garden responds in their own private way, each person identifies with something inside them that the garden evokes.

For me, spending time with Wendy, watching her strive to create the Secret Garden and being able to tell its story, has been a constant pleasure, and a reaffirming of the strong affinity I've always felt with nature and gardens from my own childhood.

Parts of my mother's garden always felt magical, and I've seen over and again how the magical vitality in Wendy's Secret Garden has inspired visitors' imaginations, and lit up their hearts. It is a great gift.

Likewise, it's been a constant pleasure to spend time with the garden's extended family, Ruben, Corrado, all the younger gardeners, and all the characters and friends involved in the Whiteley household.

We all hope that, by documenting the full story of Wendy's Secret Garden in this book, we will help to bolster its plea to allow it to remain a permanent public haven, forever more.

September 16th, 2015.

Dear Premier Baird,

I am sending this parcel, the Secret Garden Book and a tape of The Australian Story aired last week on Monday A.B.C. in the hope that you will accept an invitation to visit Lavender Bay.

I would love you and your family to come for tea at my house and to see the garden. The Book and tape are a great introduction, but nothing is as good as the real place. I have been waiting for years to approach the right person in the government — I hope youre it, and can find time.

Best wishes with the new government.

Sincerely
Wendy Whiteley.

Postscript

It was a handwritten note from Wendy Whiteley to the then NSW Premier Mike Baird, inviting him to come to tea and visit her garden, along with an advance copy of this big new beautiful book, that finally did it.

On 16 September, 2015, Wendy sent her note, this book, and a disc of *Australian Story* (see below) to our nature and beach-loving new Premier. We'd hoped that if he actually came to see the garden, as well as looking through the book, he might be touched by its unique magic, and this could be a first small step in the mammoth task of permanently saving the garden.

The next day an email arrived from the Premier's media secretary saying that the Premier was keen to visit, and a date would be set. We heard nothing more that month.

The local North Sydney Council had been trying to knock on various government doors for over a decade, to even get a meeting to discuss saving the Secret Garden, but they had gotten nowhere.

However, the stars had now aligned in a way we'd never dared dream. Wheels began turning behind the scenes in government at an amazing pace; without our knowledge, officials were scrutinising every millimetre of Wendy's Secret Garden.

The prestigious documentary program, ABC TV's *Australian Story*, had screened 'Wendy's Way', based on our book, on 7 September. It attracted a top-rating audience of 1.4 million viewers. More people watched replays, and posted messages on social media.

At the start of October, Wendy received a message that Premier Baird wished to make a private visit at 9.45 am on 9 October.

On 7 October, North Sydney Council representatives were suddenly called into a high-level government meeting and told that a 30 year lease with a rollover to a second 30 year lease would be granted, and a trust established to secure the ongoing care of the Secret Garden, maintaining Wendy's vision.

This was to be officially announced in Wendy's Secret Garden at noon on 9 October. A full media alert would be issued. The Minister for Transport and Infrastructure, Andrew Constance, the chief executive of Sydney Trains (formerly RailCorp), Howard Collins, the local Member, Jillian Skinner MP, and Mayor Jilly Gibson, would all be there.

At 9.30 am, Wendy was still upstairs wrapping her hair in a scarf, Keny was in the kitchen ready with tea, coffee and almond croissants. Ruben and Corrado were looking out for the Premier.

Within minutes Premier Baird was hopping up the stairs to Wendy's front door; tall, fit, a boyish grin on his suntanned face from years surfing at his local Manly Beach.

Over morning tea, the Premier told Wendy he'd borrowed a Brett Whiteley painting from the Art Gallery of New South Wales to hang in his office. Fittingly, it's one of Brett's *Wave* series painted in Lavender Bay in 1973–74.

Premier Baird admitted he'd heard about Wendy's Secret Garden but had never visited it. When he read the book, understood the full story and grasped the significance and scope of the Secret Garden, he loved the whole concept.

After a leisurely walk through the garden with Wendy, stopping to talk to early morning visitors along the way, he came back inside the house and stood on the famous Whiteley balcony

NSW Premier Mike Baird telling Wendy that he had decided the government would save the Secret Garden.

283

From left to right, Howard Collins, Sydney Trains chief executive; author Janet Hawley; North Sydney Mayor Jilly Gibson, Wendy Whiteley, Jillian Skinner local MP; Andrew Constance, Minister for Transport and Infrastructure.

overlooking magnificent Lavender Bay with the sun gleaming on Sydney Harbour.

'We often take Sydney Harbour for granted,' Premier Baird observed, 'we don't appreciate the harbour and the foreshores as much as we should.

'That's why saving Wendy's Garden was an easy decision for us to make, because it's the right thing to do. No one who has experienced Wendy's Garden could imagine anything taking its place.

'This garden is a gift of Wendy's to the people of Sydney – it truly is a living Whiteley that is bursting with life and creativity.

'I'm delighted that a place which brings such joy to residents and visitors, has now been secured for future generations to enjoy.'

At the noon announcement, Minister Constance declared, 'Wendy has poured her blood, sweat and tears into the garden, and she, along with the people of Sydney, deserve certainty that it will be here for years to come. Our announcement today ends the question mark over the garden's future.'

Wendy, beaming, told the assembled media, 'I'm delighted because it will become a collaboration now, instead of me having a slightly worrying feeling that somebody could arrive with a bulldozer or chainsaws and it could all be gone overnight.'

As we headed back up to the house Wendy spotted a patch of weeds growing beside a rock, spoiling her composition, and started pulling out handfuls of stickyweed. Offending weeds removed, Wendy turned to me, 'I think I'll go upstairs to my bedroom now, and have a rest, and contemplate what's finally happened today. I'm thrilled,' she smiled warmly. 'I'm truly thrilled.'

More factors have evolved since, strengthening the Secret Garden's permanent future. In 2018, the NSW Government placed a State Heritage listing over the Whiteley house and visual curtilage, protecting the views across Lavender Bay and its parklands which inspired numerous iconic Brett Whiteley paintings and drawings. The listing includes the land where Wendy has made the Secret Garden.

The NSW Heritage Council Chair, Stephen Davies, described the listing as 'very welcome and very unusual. It represents not only a beautiful place and important building, but also the story of the lives and creativity of the people who lived in that house.'

NSW Heritage Minister, Gabrielle Upton, added, 'This place is an important part of our State and nation's artistic and cultural history, and it has now been officially recognised and protected.'

Wendy remarked, aptly, 'You cannot control from the grave, not completely. You can try. But after that, it's up to other people to love beautiful places, and keep them safe.'

Wendy's Secret Garden is now internationally famous, visitors come from all over Australia and world-wide, to experience this unique garden Wendy created like a giant painting. It's become a thriving haven for community arts. Artists, sculptors, musicians, writers, film makers, fashion designers, dancers, poets, and students join art and garden lovers to seek contemplation and inspiration there.

It's often called Australia's Sissinghurst due to the highly personal link with the woman who created it.

Wendy, aged 82 at the time of writing, has paid for almost everything for 30 years, and is anxious for the garden to live on in perpetuity for everyone's enjoyment and inspiration.

A Garden Trust has been established to help fund the ongoing meticulous care and maintenance by a dedicated team of skilled gardeners. It's administered by North Sydney Council. Donations are welcome.

Account name: Wendy Whiteley Secret Garden Trust

BSB: 062 217

Account number: 10861672

Website link: www.northsydney.nsw.gov.au/donatetoWSG

More information, and how to become a volunteer, see Wendy's Secret Garden's website:

www.wendyssecretgarden.org.au

Acknowledgements

I would like to thank Wendy, her close friends, and her long-time gardeners Corrado and Ruben, for openly trusting me to write this book on a subject so dear to all their hearts.

This made going about it a far easier and more enjoyable task than it might otherwise have been.

Likewise I thank Publishing Director Julie Gibbs and Senior Editor Nicole Abadee, for the freedom to go off and write this book the way I felt it should be written. My thanks continue to Julie, Nicole, and Publishing Manager Katrina O'Brien, for so carefully nurturing the raw manuscript through all the essential stages, till it became a printed book.

Bountiful thanks to Daniel New, Lantern Books Art Director, for often sweating blood as he, Wendy and I sat around her kitchen table discussing and dissecting his flow of imaginative ideas on the book's design, layout, choice of images – and coming up with a truly splendid result.

More bountiful thanks to this book's principal photographer, Jason Busch, for his sensitive creativity and constant enthusiasm over eighteen months. Gardens are not easy to photograph, especially Wendy's Secret Garden.

Both Jason and I enjoyed several delightful chance encounters in the garden. A chat with a friendly stranger on a bench led to Jason fulfilling his wish – to fly over the Secret Garden and shoot aerials to pinpoint its magnificent location on Sydney Harbour.

Chris Joscelyne, resting on the bench, told Jason that a kind-hearted mate from his army days owned a helicopter. Chris contacted his mate Peter Clisdell, who provided his helicopter and organised another good mate, Mark McNicol, to pilot the chopper.

John Chetham, of JCa Landscape Architects, across the road from Wendy's Secret Garden, provided invaluable help by mapping the Secret Garden. John cheerfully took on the epic jigsaw puzzle task, which had driven many others bonkers. With survey and graphic assistance from four of his staff, John successfully completed a ground map of the garden, as well as plotting its boundaries onto Jason's aerial photographs.

Dr Ian Hoskins, North Sydney Council Historian, and author of *Sydney Harbour: A history* provided generous help as I gathered written and pictorial material for this book's historical chapter (chapter 5).

Thanks also to North Sydney Council for assistance from the Historical Services team at the North Sydney Heritage Centre/Stanton Library, providing historical illustrations of Lavender Bay.

The indefatigable Lou Klepac and his son Mal Damkar of the Beagle Press, are thanked for assisting with images of some Brett Whiteley drawings. Joanna Collard, picture researcher and Wendy's long-time friend, proved a blessing with her skills in sourcing early family photographs and images of artworks.

My gratitude to Garry Shead, Peter Kingston and Michael Hobbs for the use of images from their wondrous 1973 film *Fanta*. And again to Kingo for his evocative Lavender Bay etching.

Photographer Tim Bauer kindly provided favourite photographs of Wendy and her friends that he took in 2006 when Tim worked with me on the original magazine story.

William Yang and Greg Weight dug out wonderful photographs they took of Brett and Wendy during their Lavender Bay years together. Ian MacTavish loaned Box Brownie photographs of Brett from his childhood.

My grateful thanks to so many others who shared early photographs and memories, including Made Wijaya, Graham Jepson, Jim Anderson, Peter Muller, Helen Simons and Stuart Purves, gardeners, especially Chantal and Nick, and visitors. Barry Pearce's son, Alyosha, took a lovely photograph of his father.

Special thanks to Keny for her always warm, welcoming smile, calmly efficient manner, and offer to make coffee as soon as I arrive inside Wendy's home. Thanks to all the younger gardeners on the Secret Garden team, for their obvious dedication.

This dedication is also regularly displayed by the Volunteers, a fine group of locals who weed and generally help out where the senior gardeners direct.

Much credit is due to Robert Emerson, Director of Open Spaces and Environmental Services at North Sydney Council, for his long-held faith in the immense value that Wendy's Secret Garden has added to the community, and his ongoing work to help preserve the garden's present and future life.

Thanks to Fiona Inglis, my literary agent, for guiding me through the maze of publishers who wanted to publish this book, and helping with the difficult decision of who would handle it best. Along that journey I very much want to thank Helen Littleton for her long belief in this book, and for the opening line in the final chapter.

On a more personal note, I want to thank my brother Grant Hawley for our lifetime of shared love of nature and gardens, instilled into us largely by our mother Margot Hawley, and helped along by our father Arthur. This shared love is continued with Grant's wife, Dr Wendy Craik.

My heartfelt thanks to my son Ben Petinsky, a landscape gardener in Bangalow, northern New South Wales, for always sharing his passionate love of nature and gardens with me and many others. And to my nature-loving advertising guru daughter Kim Petinsky, for her endless wise advice on design, creativity, human behaviour and all else in life.

To my partner, architect Philip Cox, thank you for the decades of conversations, insights and precious times spent together in gardens, both here and in our travels around the globe.

Impressions from the Photographer

Jason Busch

Peering through the old glass bricks built into our fireplace as a five-year-old, I can still remember seeing the fairies of my childhood secret garden, playing amongst the branches of the blackberry bushes and the fractured afternoon light. I hadn't thought of this as an adult until I walked a zigzag path into Wendy Whiteley's Secret Garden.

There are no complete overviews of the garden; the line of sight is tempted away constantly by half-views and the promise of more around the next bend. Veils of leaves obscure, paths twist and curl along the high-sided garden wall or hang from the edge of Clark Park and drop steeply into the green cover below. Wendy, Corrado, Jay Jay and Ruben are constantly handcrafting rails, moving plants and building stone walls that look to a design as elusive and complex as the mesh of leaves above.

The sunlight is focused into hard beams of light by the tall buildings that surround the garden and make opportunities to photograph the space as fleeting as the small birds and insects that occupy the dense undergrowth. Light shafts pierce the garden so intensely that the leaves become x-rays of themselves, veins criss-cross in relief. Plumes of vibrant red flare as if they might have caught on fire, insects and the moist breath of plants fill the air with movement, exposed for a moment then hidden again by the deep shadow that follows.

Climb down to the floor of the garden and it is easy to forget the storybook views of Sydney Harbour. The bright panoramas of Clark Park, the leafy views of the Sydney Harbour Bridge and Luna Park have gone. The garden gathers itself here, leans in and becomes a single swath of green, hiding the map of pathways and the people drawn to this private space. Here there is room to run and explore, to contemplate and sleep protected beneath the arc of the garden.

There is no simple signature to the design; too many details to connect and frame for a single story. At times it can seem impenetrable, a maze of plants and dead ends. At other times it leads you around until the last light of the day – watching, waiting, promising one more glance of golden light to fill the garden with life. Wait and wait until the darkness surrounds you completely and the mosquitoes drive you to the top. As you climb the stairs you return to a larger view of the night sky and a horizon of city lights sparkling on the water.

Complex and irregular, it does not observe the order I am used to photographing; it holds its nature close. The plants have history as purposeful as the objects and art that have been placed amongst them – this is a garden that has been loved for a long time. There is something special in this space for me, the minutiae and grand old trees sit as comfortable companions, and I find my childhood memories can as well.

Photographic and artwork credits

PENGUIN BOOKS

UK | USA | Canada | Ireland | Australia
India | New Zealand | South Africa | China

Penguin Books is part of the Penguin Random House group of companies
whose addresses can be found at global.penguinrandomhouse.com

First published by Lantern in 2015
This revised edition published by Penguin Books in 2023

Cover and text design by Daniel New © Penguin Group (Australia)
Typeset in Fairfield

Printed and bound in China

 A catalogue record for this
book is available from the
National Library of Australia

Creator: Hawley, Janet, 1944- author.
Title: Wendy Whiteley and the secret garden / Janet Hawley ;
photography by Jason Busch.

ISBN 978 1 76134 432 9

penguin.com.au